Tools for Collaborative Decision-Making

FOCUS SERIES IN COMPUTER ENGINEERING AND IT

Series Editor Jean-Charles Pomerol

Tools for Collaborative Decision-Making

Pascale Zaraté

First published 2013 in Great Britain and the United States by ISTE Ltd and John Wiley & Sons, Inc.

ISTE Ltd
27-37 St George's Road
London SW19 4EU
UK

www.iste.co.uk

John Wiley & Sons, Inc.
111 River Street
Hoboken, NJ 07030
USA

www.wiley.com

Library of Congress Control Number: 2012949420

British Library Cataloguing-in-Publication Data
A CIP record for this book is available from the British Library
ISSN: 2051-2481 (Print)
ISSN: 2051-249X (Online)
ISBN: 978-1-84821-516-0

Printed and bound in Great Britain by CPI Group (UK) Ltd., Croydon, Surrey CR0 4YY

Contents

Figures

Tables

Introduction

Decision support uses techniques and methods drawn from applied mathematics – such as optimization, statistics and decision theory – and theories from less formal domains such as organizational analysis and cognitive sciences.

While their work has had less of a normative impact than has decision theory, Roy and Bouyssou [ROY 93] view decision support as a science based on three main postulates:

– first order reality postulate: the main aspects of the reality on which decision support is founded relate to knowledge objects – objects which can be regarded as facts, stable enough that we can speak of the exact state or exact value of one or other of their characteristics: a value deemed to have significance in relation to an aspect of the reality;

– decision-maker postulate: for every decision, there is a decision-maker: a clearly identified and fully competent actor, obeying a rational system of preferences in the sense of a set of axioms that prevent ambiguity and incomparability, which the decision support does not attempt to alter;

– optimum postulate: in any situation where a decision must be made, there is at least one optimal decision, for which it can be proven that there is no obviously better solution, and which is equitable in terms of the decision-making process.

Roy and Bouyssou hold that people's ability to abstractly represent phenomena and their capacity for hypothetical-deductive reasoning can be – and are – used in the service of action: the person reflects before intervening, constructing a scenario in his/her head before acting.

Such deduction and modeling, when consciously exercised with a view to enlightening a person's behavior during a decision-making process, is the very essence of decision support.

Roy and Bouyssou define decision support as the activity of someone (a researcher) who, using clearly expressed and reasonably well formalized models, seeks to partially answer the questions which an actor (decision-maker) asks him/herself during the decision-making process. These partial answers, when combined, help illuminate the decision, and normally suggest a certain course of action to help ensure the process is more compatible with the actor's goals and guiding values system.

Furthermore, they stress that decision support helps participants in the decision-making process to be constructive, sit down together and share their various convictions. It ensures that there is room for critical discussion to take place, regarding the basis for the decision and how it is taken.

According to Tsoukias [TSO 08], there are a number of approaches to decision support: normative, descriptive, prescriptive and constructive. Regardless of which approach is taken, he considers decision support to be a process involving:

– at least two participants: the client and the analyst;

– at least two objectives: the client's concerns and the analyst's motivations;

– a set of resources including the client's knowledge about the matter of concern, the analyst's methodological knowledge, and time;

– an object of convergence (a meta-object), which is a shared representation of the client's concerns.

He views decision support as a distributed cognitive process. He also puts forward a set of artifacts generated by the decision support process.

In order to provide decision support as effectively as possible, we must develop software tools.

Numerous systems have been created with the aim of providing the best possible decision support, while fitting into decision support frameworks as fully as possible. These systems are not always used to their full extent. In large organizations, spreadsheet applications are still very widely used for operational level decisions and tactical management decisions.

However, the introduction of information and communication technology (ICT) has considerably altered the process of decision-making in organizations. This is our working hypothesis, to which Chapter 1 is devoted.

Based on this working hypothesis, in Chapter 2, we present our investigation of this new context of decision-making. The change in the process is related to the switch from a context where there is a single decision-maker to one where there are multiple decision-makers, operating separately and independently, where the various decision-makers need to cooperate.

It is useful to define exactly what it is that we mean by "cooperation". This concept is analyzed in Chapter 3.

Chapter 4 defines and discusses a newly-emerging concept: cooperative decision-making. We present a generic model of this concept.

In order to provide decision support for use in these new cooperative processes, we must develop new tools.

We begin Chapter 5 by defining systems to support decision-making in a fairly general sense. Several types of systems will be described: decision support systems (DSSs), intelligent DSSs (IDSSs), cooperative knowledge-based systems, cooperative systems, group decision support systems, business intelligence, collaborative engineering, workflows and cooperative multi-agent systems. We also show in this chapter how the work of certain key users such as facilitators can be supported, and how an approach of collaborative design of all these systems can be drawn up.

Throughout this chapter, we illustrate how these previously-developed systems, which have been in use for some time, no longer satisfy current requirements.

Finally, in Chapter 6, we demonstrate collaborative decision support systems (CDSSs). Basically, these are software suites that can assist collaborative decision-making. The essential characteristic of these packages, which sets them apart from the systems defined previously, is interactive planning of cooperation between the various actors.

Such planning is possible thanks to various tools, either derived from artificial intelligence (AI) or from operational research and linear programming.

Cooperative decision support systems are considered as a platform or toolbox, including various tools such as:

– an interpersonal communication tool;

– a task management tool;

– a knowledge capitalization tool;

– a dynamic man/machine interaction tool.

The usefulness of these different tools is demonstrated in a separate section given over to each of them.

1

Alteration of Decision-Making Processes in Organizations

The concept of decision-making in organizations has been very widely studied, and numerous definitions have been put forward. To help define this concept more precisely, we can cite the following authors.

According to Le Moigne [LEM 74], to make a decision is to identify and solve the problems that any organization will inevitably face.

We can also cite Kast [KAS 93], for whom decision-making is synonymous with choosing between several existing alternatives, each with different consequences. The selection is made in accordance with very precise criteria.

Stal [STA 00] holds that a decision is a process which leads an actor to answer a given question.

For Longueville [LON 03], decision-making is a process of information transformation. It leads an actor or group of actors within the organization to deal with an issue, giving rise to an action.

Thus, decision-making can be simplified as the choice of an option from a set of alternatives by an actor or a group of actors in response to a problem faced by an organization, with this choice being guided by a number of very precise criteria.

1.1. Decisional processes

In reality, this is a complex activity, which a number of authors have suggested should be defined and modeled as a process; thus, we define the decisional process, which generally comprises several stages.

For Simon [SIM 77] the process is made up of the following stages:

– intelligence: this is a cognitive process that involves gathering information about the problem at hand, its constraints and its environment;

– design: this is a stage of designing, developing and analyzing solutions to deal with the problem;

– choice: the choice of the solution is adopted here in view of the criteria developed and adopted in the previous stage;

– review: at this stage, the previous stages are re-examined – i.e. the decision-maker continues to look for information whilst designing a solution to the problem in a continually looping process.

Furthermore, Simon describes this process as being neither linear nor sequential; the "review" stage is ever-present in the mind of the decision-maker, who refines the criteria guiding the decision while continuing to look for information and construct possible solutions.

Courbon [COU 82] also defines this process as being cyclical, so the solution can be readjusted as the process advances.

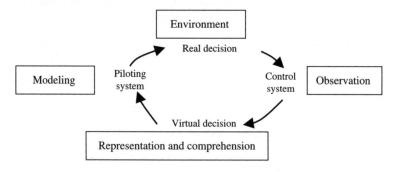

Figure 1.1. *Courbon's decision-making process [COU 82]*

The specific characteristic of Stal's model [STA 00] is that it considers a multi-actor process. She puts forward a multi-actor model of decision-making called the DTL (decision time line). This process is made up of several stages, at which any of the actors can intervene.

Lavergne [LAV 83] proposes a six-stage breakdown of the decision-making process:

1) definition: the object of the decision, the context and the ethics are defined;

2) information: the decision-maker looks for and gathers information useful for the decision;

3) analysis: at this stage, the decision-maker organizes all the pertinent information gathered;

4) solution: at this stage, the actor designs and concretizes the hypotheses for the making of the decision;

5) determination: a choice is made by weighing up the hypotheses, the possible consequences and the ethical constraints;

6) implementation: the decision is applied in concrete terms.

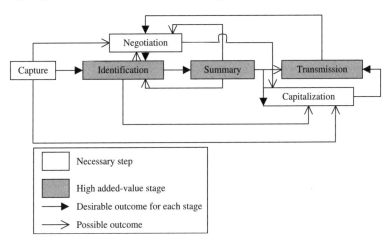

Figure 1.2. *DTL (decision time line) [STA 00]*

This process has the peculiarity of including the implementation of the decision-making process.

The originality of Cauvin's model [CAU 05] lies in the fact that it actually takes account of the process of knowledge capitalization in the decision-making process.

All these models of decisional processes exhibit certain common characteristics:

– they all comprise multiple stages;

– they may involve single or multiple actors;

– in the more recent models, a process of knowledge capitalization is coupled with the decisional process.

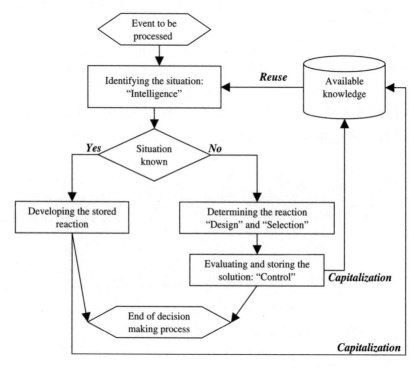

Figure 1.3. *Cauvin's decisional process [CAU 05]*

In this chapter, our aim is to show how the processes of decision-making in organizations are currently evolving. This observation will serve as a base from which to demonstrate how the tools hitherto developed and used must evolve in order to better serve the needs of a changing society.

1.2. Introduction of ICT in organizations

Tétard [TÉT 02] showed that the introduction of ICT into organizations inevitably leads to fragmentation of working time. He also showed that information overload is both a source and a consequence of this fragmentation. Given that humans have limited cognitive capacities, we must attempt to reduce this excess workload, using appropriate tools.

In addition, with the advent of ICT, the classic DSSs become partially usable, although only when the group of decision-makers comes together. We then witness a reinforcement of the collaborative work between different actors involved in the decision-making process.

In collaborative work, it is crucial to model the cooperation. The goal is to encourage shared work. The processes of cooperation then take center stage, regardless of the goals of the task.

The need of businesses to remain reactive and the technological evolution are leading to wide-reaching changes in the organizational and cognitive processes.

Organizational processes are evolving and tending towards having more parties involved in the making of decisions: the responsibilities and the initiative tend to be more distributed.

On the other hand, the necessity to report and inform becomes a generalized imperative. A large proportion of a manager's actions consists of securing the participation of and motivating as many of the actors concerned as possible.

Even when the organizational responsibility for the decision is assumed by a single person, the decision is almost always prepared through collaborative work. Processes of cooperation increase; they play an increasingly important part in decision-making, because the situations dictate that it be so. In particular, two fundamental conditions of cooperation are encouraged by this evolution:

– Intensification of interactions: because of this, there is an increased potential for cooperative behaviors, and these behaviors do indeed increase (see Axelrod [AXE 92] and Delahaye [DEL 95]).

– Intensification of exchanges: this means players are better able to apprehend the other players' goals, which is also a significant factor in establishing cooperative behavior (see [ZAC 90]).

The organizational context is omnipresent in decision-making. It forms an integral part of individual decisions by empowerment of the individual actor; this, in itself, is an integral part of collective decisions. By definition, organizational decisions build up the organization, but they also determine its actions. The consequence is that decision-making is often a diffuse process in collective and organizational activity. Decisions are constructed gradually, circulating through different "arenas" of exchange between actors. When the decision is taken, in a manner of speaking, a change in the organizational state takes place.

In collective activity, the process of decision-making also provides a forum for negotiations between the actors involved in it. In this to-and-fro that Simon [SIM 77] calls problem setting/problem solving, where the problem is reformulated constantly to the point where it can easily be solved, until it reaches an intermediary state which is close to the final state, there is negotiation between the actors about the way in which to pose the problem, and contrasting of the different ways in which it could be posed.

Indeed, it is strategically advantageous, from everyone's point of view, to clarify the terms in which the problem is posed in different ways – notably by using contextual elements which have a bearing on the definition of the problem, and on the quantifiable consequences of certain choices.

All these aspects suggest that we not only need to review our model of decision-making, but to redesign the decision support which we offer, focusing on three essential elements: the plethora of information, the importance that must be attached to the processes of innovation and design, and finally relativization of the choice stage and introduction of negotiation and other collective processes.

An actor within the organization is placed in a new situation, which is characterized by very easy access to information (to a plethora of information, even), increased participation in many proceedings, meetings and groups spanning various levels of the organization. She/he therefore has to deal with shorter time-periods in which to take a stand on a given issue, and a set of situations which frequently lead to "cognitive overflow syndrome" (see Lahlou [LAH 00]).

Of the various cognitive processes which are becoming essential for dealing with new situations, we can cite relevance selection and the vigilance which this involves. The relevance of a fact is perceived by an individual based on the strong reactions that it arouses in him or her (see Sperber and Wilson [SPE 90]). Thus, it is a quality of the object which is evaluated on the basis of the effect it has on the subject who perceives it. As we can see from this standpoint, cognition is thought of as being "situated". The need to perceive relevance requires a great deal of involvement of the part of the individual, in relation to his/her task and to the organization.

Indeed, in order to quickly perceive what is relevant for the company, individuals must have an in-depth knowledge of its interests, needs and outlooks. The more relevant a fact is, the less cognitive effort is needed. Vigilance is a deliberate state of mind on the part of the actor, which increases his/her chances of perceiving the relevant elements around him/her.

In order to perceive the relevance of information and capitalize on the opportunities which they may represent for the company, the actor must exercise vigilance.

1.3. The decision-making process revisited

Based on these initial observations, we propose to revisit the canonic model of decision-making put forward by Simon, on the understanding that we shall still use this framework to model an actor's thought process, which takes place within a tenth of a second [SIM 77]. We have just described this model, and it can be summarized thus: with the environment changing more quickly, each actor has to increase his/her vigilance and watchfulness. Of the phases distinguished by Simon (Figure 1.4), the intelligence phase becomes more active and more complex, because the environment which has to be taken into account in that phase is more complex. Yet the way in which that environment is "read" is also altered: the actor has an increased role in looking for relevance. Whereas previously, he/she had to search through elements of information so as not to overlook any that were important, he/she now has to perform lightning-quick filtering of a plethora of information. The design phase also takes place more often, because each visit to the environment involves evaluating the relevance.

The choice phase, it seems, is not greatly altered, given that, in the ultra-quick process described above, there is no real generation of similar alternatives and systematic comparison and selection of one of these alternatives by a rational process of evaluation and reasoning.

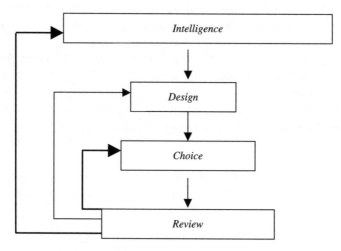

Figure 1.4. *The progression of Simon's phases of decision-making [SIM 77] revisited*

Hence, the progression of the loop is altered (Figure 1.4): the first two phases are visited more often than the third. The review loopback from the choice stage to the intelligence stage is reinforced, but so too is the loopback from design to intelligence. Many iterations of this cycle take place before making a choice or even *thinking* about making a choice. The previous model – whereby information is sought in order to present several possible solutions in a "design" phase geared towards the making of a choice – is evolving toward an emerging vision where running over the available information without preconceptions gives rise to alternatives, one or other of which will occasionally be decided upon. Whilst not departing from Simon's model, in a way, we run through the loop differently, and the processes which each phase covers have changed. It is important not to view the sequentiality of this model as anything more than a device to help thinking – as Simon himself pointed out.

We shall also take from this that the changes in the organizational and cognitive processes occur simultaneously, and in a causal and interlinked manner (for further details, see Teulier and Zaraté [TEU 01]).

In addition, Pomerol and Adam [POM 04] showed that not only did Simon's research have a profound impact on the domain of information systems, but also, although he did not work directly on decision support systems, he greatly influenced the design of such systems. Indeed, they showed that his contribution regarding the process of decision-making, the principle of limited rationality and the connections between decision-making, organization and management, is of vital importance in the domain of the decision support systems which we shall describe in Chapter 5.

1.4. Conclusion

The work cited above has shown that the processes of decision-making in organizations have evolved from a cognitive point of view. Indeed, beginning with Simon's model, we have shown that there is a strengthening of the feedback loops from the last phase – review – back to the choice and intelligence phases. This process has also evolved in organizational terms. We have gone from the context of a single decision-maker to an environment with multiple decision-makers, who can work in synchronization or not, and apart or together. Hence, it is necessary to analyze these particular modes of decision-making. This is the topic of the next chapter.

2

New Decision-Making Processes

Having put in place the basic premise for our discussion, in this chapter we examine the process of decision-making in the particular context with multiple decision-makers. Indeed, before we can create software tools to support these new decision-making processes, we must first gain an understanding of how they are constructed and how decision-makers operate within this framework.

2.1. Examination of the context of such decision-making

In most organizations, the vast majority of decisions are taken after intensive consultation with numerous people, rather than by individual decision-makers working in larger organizations (see Gory and Scott Morton [GOR 71]). In addition, [GOR 71] showed that the more complex the organization becomes, the less the decisions are taken by lone individuals. According to Smoliar and Sprague [SMO 02], decision-making processes in organizations generally involve several actors, interacting with one another. This interaction implies communication of information and an understanding shared by the decision-makers involved in these processes. They analyze this interaction from three different angles: the meaning of the information being handled must be the same for all the actors involved; the authority necessary for an agent – human or artificial – to be able to regulate workloads; and finally the confidence that the users can have in the various forms of technology, which, notably, may involve different visual representations of the shared knowledge.

The participants in a decision-making process must pool their efforts and work towards a common goal, where they have to integrate multiple points of view which may not necessarily be compatible. They have to work together, although not necessarily in the same place or at the same time. They are committed to a coordination effort in order to solve the problem, where they have to divide the task of making the decision into different sub-tasks which will be assigned to individual players.

A number of authors have analyzed the process of group decision-making from various different perspectives, but without really introducing the notion of context, which must be taken into account when developing decision support tools. It is also noteworthy that these analyses are carried out from the viewpoint of various disciplines – particularly that of social psychology. In this context, let us cite the work of MacGrath [MAC 84], who showed that the behavior of groups is difficult to analyze accurately. The notion of the working context must also be taken into account. He also shows that it is also necessary to comprehend the nature of the task set for the group and its characteristics.

We are particularly interested in the work of Marakas [MAR 03], for whom the process of group decision-making must be analyzed from five perspectives: the structure of the group, the roles within that group, the group's processes, the group's style and the group's norms. We believe this analysis to be pertinent in that it offers a definition of the context of group work.

The structure of the group: [MAR 03] defines this by different sorts of structures depending on the number of people and the type of group: an individual, a team with a notion of hierarchy, a committee which requires consensus amongst its members, or a less structured group;

The roles within that group: each member of the group may assume one or more specific roles (e.g. analyst, user of the DSS, etc.);

The group's processes: the processes used for decision-making can have a considerable influence on the outcome of the decision. Indeed, the processes of circulation of the flow of information or decision are generally well known and can be analyzed in the form of workflow, for instance; the way in which the process has to converge is generally not explicit, which can sway the decision in one direction or another. Does a consensus have to be reached? If so, is there a certain time-limit on the process?

The group's style: the style of a decision-maker can affect the process, the group's behavior in certain circumstances as well as the quality of the expectations of the decision;

The group's norms: this is probably the most important dimension. The social psychology of decision-making accords a particular importance to norms.

It is important to be attentive to the existence of a meaning shared by the participants, to collective or individual social pressures, to genres (male/female balance) and to prescriptions relating to the group's behavior, personal behaviors and potential sanctions, which together make up the decision-making environment.

According to Brézillon [BRÉ 03], a knowledge base shared between the members of the group is constructed dynamically, which involves proceduralization of the context – i.e. activation of part of the general context of the task being performed, by way of interactions between different individuals. Furthermore, [BRE 03a] defines a different granularity of the context depending on the focus of the task or decision-making. In particular, he shows that the context of the taking of a decision is dynamic, and varies depending on whether we observe the group in its totality or a series of different individuals or simply the context of the project.

Jankovic [JAN 06] showed that the notion of collaborative decision-making is very relevant in the field of project management. She proposes to apprehend this notion from four viewpoints, so as to support collaborative decision-making using a project management approach.

Séguy [SÉG 08] showed that the notion of collaborative decision-making has become a very important concept in the domain of e-maintenance. Indeed, she points out that "the maintenance function has been strongly penetrated by ICTs with, for example, the concepts of telemaintenance or e-maintenance. The introduction of ICTs into maintenance has shifted the working modes of maintenance operators toward a larger collaboration, which has revolutionized exchanges, working conditions, decision-making..."

In order to better comprehend these new processes of decision-making, it is necessary to study the context in which they take place.

2.2. Context and decision-making

Brézillon *et al.* [BRÉ 03b] published a case study, relating to the publication of a daily and a weekly newspaper in Ireland. They showed that the introduction of information and communication technology into this enterprise greatly modified the process of production, thereby improving the company's productivity. We have analyzed this case study in accordance with the analysis dimensions defined by Marakas, and showed that the introduction of ICT for decision-making involves an alteration of the structure of the group:

– *The structure* becomes more diffuse; the group is generally constructed in an ephemeral manner, without there being genuine formalization of its structure. The group does not know whether it is structured as a team, a committee or as a hierarchical entity.

– *The group's style* includes different styles stemming from the various groups making up the decision-making group; as the group is only set up for a specific need, the members do not really have enough time for a clear style of the group to emerge.

– *The norms* exhibit the same phenomenon as the group's *processes*; they come from different groups and are therefore mixed in with one another.

– *The roles* within the group include various roles relating to the different groups; a member of the group creates his/her own role, which may be a mixture of roles that he/she has played previously in other groups.

We also showed that the dynamics of the context of decision-making, under the influence of ICT, is more reactive and more volatile. The cognitive workload of the decision-makers is greater, because they share a larger amount of information and must therefore remember more information (see Brézillon and Zaraté [BRÉ 08]).

When creating any cooperative decision support systems, we believe it is essential to take account of the context of the study or at least the study of the context when drawing up the specifications of the system to be created.

In order to validate the theoretical study of the context, an experiment was carried out thanks to the competition and collaboration of a number of university students from INP Toulouse.

2.3. Experiment

In this section, we present an experiment which we carried out in collaboration with a number of engineering students. To begin this section, we wish to extend our thanks to those students, because without their goodwill and commitment, this study could never have come to fruition.

The experiment was defined as follows. The students were asked to take a decision in a group of 10, first in synchronous, non-distributed mode, around a table; they were then asked to take a similar decision in asynchronous and non-distributed mode; and finally to take a third decision in asynchronous distributed mode. In all three cases, they had the multicriteria decision support program CooP, developed by Tung Bui [BUI 87], at their disposal. The tool includes a number of methods for multicriteria decision support: Promethee, Saaty, Electre and Weighted Sum. The students could only use two methods – Electre and the weighted sum, because those are the only methods that they had studied. The system can be used in asynchronous mode, distributed or otherwise. It also enables the user to define an area of negotiation between the decision-makers and see whether a consensus has been reached. The decisions needing to be taken are different from one experiment to the next. In the first case, the simulation was of recruitment of one person out of three candidates for a company, based on five previously-defined criteria. In the second and third cases, the challenge was to award a grant to one student out of three, going to spend their final year of study abroad. Obviously, the students described in situations two and three were different. However, the criteria to be taken into account were the same and were also defined previously.

The problems were defined in such a way that the decision to be taken is not obvious. Each of the 10 decision-makers had the same weighting as everyone else, for all three situations. We do not see significant effects of learning, despite the similarity of the tasks; at least this effect, if it exists, was only marginally taken into account in the analysis.

For the first experiment, in face-to-face mode, the students first discussed the situations around the table, and then gradually, each one of them formed their own opinion. When they felt ready, they were able to express their own preference in the CooP system installed in the board room. We were on hand to help them if need be, and the task lasted the duration of a normal seminar period. We gave them clarifications about the problem needing to be dealt with and about how to use the CooP system; we played the role of project managers, but without communicating to them our own decisions. They were filmed and recorded. At the end of the session, the problems relating to experiments two and three were handed out to them, along with a questionnaire to fill in.

For the second experiment, the students were asked to come at their convenience to mark their own preference on the computer in that same boardroom before a given deadline.

For the third experiment, they went at their convenience to mark their respective preferences on different computers in different computer rooms before the same deadline. In addition, they had to return the completed questionnaire before that deadline.

In terms of multicriteria analysis of the three problems to be solved, it was a question of choice, not classification or sorting (for further details, see [ROY 85]). Although this experiment was not taken into account in evaluating the "Methods and Tools for Decision Support" module that they learnt, it was a resounding success with the students: all of them responded. We can sum up the characteristics of the three experiments in the following table:

Characteristics	Experiment 1	Experiment 2	Experiment 3
Mode	The members of the group discuss the issue around a table, and give their own preference on a specific computer	The members of the group go whenever they want, to mark their own preference on the same computer	The members of the group go whenever they want, to mark their own preference on multiple computers
Structuring of the problem	Imposed by the project managers	Imposed by the project managers	Imposed by the project managers
Communication between members of the group	Imposed around the table	If they so desire	If they so desire
Type of problem	Recruitment	Assignment of a study grant	Assignment of a study grant

Table 2.1. *Table showing the characteristics of the experiments*

The questionnaire was designed to shed light on some of the questions which we were asking ourselves: is it possible for a consensus to emerge naturally in an asynchronous and distributed context? If so, have there been exchanges between the members of the group? Does each decision-maker in their own corner feel lost? Do they take an interest in one another?

Does this force them to cooperate amongst themselves? Is the efficiency of the emergence of the decision related to the number of exchanges between the decision-makers? Are there differences for the decision-makers between experiments two and three?

Generally speaking, we were able to show that the students see no difference between experiments two and three. They appear to feel no need to communicate amongst themselves, and indeed only did communicate with one another for reminders of the password to get onto the CooP program. Also, in general, our subjects said they preferred experiment one, then three, then two. It should be noted that the differences between the tasks are not significant to account for these results (see Zaraté, Soubie and Bui [ZAR 05]).

While we are aware of the limitations of this study, we believe that the asynchronous, non-distributed situation offers no flexibility in terms of the use of group decision support systems, other than to store information or knowledge in a very specific place. In addition, we believe it crucial, in group decision-making, to maintain social contact between the members of the group. Indeed, the major advantage of the "face-to-face" situation lies in the opportunity that it offers the individuals to discuss and argue their cases. The process of debate is a key stage in a negotiation process. It would be over-simplistic to symmetrically link negotiation and decision-making. Negotiation is one of the forms of decision-making, but there can be other types of decisions – choice, classification, etc. Thus, discussion and debate is essential in negotiation but is also necessary in terms of choice or classification. It allows the viewpoints of all the decision-makers to evolve more quickly. Hence, we believe that a decision-making process must be managed in the same way that a project is managed, introducing milestones and meetings in order to allow all the decision-makers to take part in the debate stage.

We were able to detect two types of bias in this experiment. The first relates to the very nature of the experiment, conducted using students whose motivation is less driven than in a real-world situation with real decision-makers in real organizations. Indeed, our experiment is merely a simulation, with all the limitations that are inherent in a non real-world situation. The second relates to the fact that between the first and third experiments, a phenomenon of learning must have taken place, enabling them to make their third decision more easily than the first.

2.4. Conclusion

We must highlight an important conclusion to this chapter, which we shall draw upon in chapters to come. When supported by increasingly advanced and sophisticated tools, decision-makers exhibit a preference for real face-to-face situations, with construction of common proceduralized knowledge in these meetings. We must also highlight another conclusion which will serve as a basis for our later discussion: the situation of making decisions in asynchronous non-distributed mode is absolutely not preferred by the decision-makers. Indeed, in terms of decision-making, there is no significant reason to apply and use this situation.

3

The Need to Cooperate

As demonstrated in Chapter 1, the cognitive and organizational processes of decision-making have evolved. We have seen an explosion of these processes, with the need for cooperation between the different actors involved in the process of decision-making that we call "cooperative decision-making". A number of actors are involved in this process, and must communicate amongst themselves, or cooperate.

Before defining new systems that are able to support cooperative decision-making, we have to define what cooperation is, along with the concepts associated with it: coordination and collaboration.

3.1. Cooperation: definitions

Schmidt and Bannon [SCH 92] propose to use the definition of cooperative work as a starting point from which to define cooperation. They characterize cooperative work as people working together, who are mutually dependent for their work and who cooperate in order to perform their task. This definition is given from the viewpoint of an outside observer of the whole system.

Also, and *a contrario*, cooperation can be defined from the point of view of each agent involved in the general process. For de Terssac and Maggi [DET 96], cooperation is the way of overcoming individual limitations. Cooperation can also be defined as the set of collective actions finalized and developed to deal with individual limitations.

Another way of framing the process of cooperation between different agents would be to define it by adopting an perspective of organizational analysis. For Hatchuel [HAT 96], cooperation is the very *raison d'être* of organizations. Cooperation is not merely a set of actions orientated towards a common goal. The process of cooperation is based on shared learning in order to enable each actor to construct their own objectives whilst interacting with their partners.

Thus, to cooperate is to explore what cooperation there can be between the partners. Hatchuel defines cooperation more in relation to each individual than in relation to the overall organization.

Human/human cooperation has long been a field of observation that serves as the basis for developing tools to help in the achievement of so-called cooperative tasks. From this standpoint, an agent must be a human being. These observations of man/man cooperation have been used as the basis for the development of cooperative systems. The cooperation should thus be able to be observed at different levels: between the human operator and the system; between the different agents making up the system; or indeed from the global point of view of the system.

According to Erschler *et al.* [ERS 93], cooperation is a (re)negotiation of constraints between different decision centers. For Erschler, an agent is seen as a decisional agent. Cooperation is then described as a process of debate between various agents – a necessary process in decision-making. Here, the degree of analysis is at the level of each agent.

From the point of view of the whole system, in order for there to be cooperation between various agents, a certain number of conditions must be fulfilled. According to Soubie [SOU 98], for there to be cooperation between different actors, there must be:

– a common goal;

– actors involved in a problem-solving process;

– communication tools;

– the tasks to be accomplished in order to solve the general problem must be separable.

Rosenthal-Sabroux [ROS 96] put forward an analysis of cooperation from four viewpoints:

– Point of view of dialog and communication (see Falzon [FAL 91] and Pavard [PAV 87]), where the cooperation between the various agents is analyzed horizontally: what are the impacts of a cooperative task on the dialog between the agents? Here, cooperation is seen between humans and the system and between the agents making up the system.

– Organizational point of view (see Mintzberg [MIN 79]), where the cooperation between the various agents is analyzed vertically: how will the agents organize themselves in order to deal with a cooperative task? Here, as in the previous point, cooperation is analyzed between humans and the system, and between the agents making up the system.

– Point of view of control of the process in supervision-type problems (see [MIL 87]), where cooperation is defined horizontally: how will the different agents, e.g. on a production line, react in relation to one another when their task changes? However, the cooperation is also analyzed vertically: how is the control of the process managed? Is there a need for cooperation between the agents involved in the production process, for instance, and the agent in control of the overall process? The three levels of analysis of the process of cooperation are present here: between humans and the system, between the various agents and from a global view of the system.

– Point of view of multi-agent distributed artificial intelligence (see Bouron [BOU 93]) – here, cooperation is analyzed from the point of view of each agent: what information is necessary for an agent to perform his/her task properly? How will they coordinate between themselves? In this scenario, the point of observation is placed at the level of the agents making up the system.

Our intention is to give a definition of cooperation which can be useful in the development of cooperative systems, integrating all three viewpoints: human/system cooperation, cooperation between different agents and cooperation from the point of view of the whole system.

Thus, we propose the following definition. Cooperation implies:

– participation of multiple agents (human or otherwise) to solve a problem: whole system point of view;

  – common objective between all the agents:

    - total: point of view of the whole system,

    - partial: point of view of the agents,

  – possession of the means of communication: point of view of the agents and point of view of human/system cooperation;

  – possession of the capacity to break the problem needing to be solved down into sub-problems: point of view of the overall system and of the agents;

  – integration of agents with skills/knowledge to carry out tasks: point of view of the agents;

  – possession of a distribution function and control of assignment of tasks to agents (allocation of resources): point of view of the whole system.

In order to ensure proper cooperation between the agents, there must be coordination and/or collaboration between them. What is the difference, though, between cooperation, collaboration and coordination?

From a point of view internal to the system, Dillenbourg *et al.* [DIL 96] state that collaboration is based on a mutual commitment of the participants in a coordinated effort to solve a given problem.

From a point of view external to the system, Menachof and Son [MEN 03] view collaboration as a framework which can be used to order different forms of cooperation between independent organizations.

We view collaboration as a degraded (less perfect) form of cooperation. Collaboration implies:

– implies the participation of multiple agents (human or otherwise) to solve a problem: point of view of the whole system;

– having a shared goal:

- total: point of view of the whole system,

- partial: point of view of the agents,

– possessing means of communication: point of view of the agents and point of view of human/system cooperation;

– each agent having skills/knowledge to carry out tasks: point of view of the agents;

– possessing capacities for breaking down the problem to be solved into sub-problems: point of view of the whole system and of the agents.

In terms of coordination, the analysis can only be performed from two points of view: the overall system and the individual agents. Indeed, it is more common to speak of man/machine *communication* than man/machine *coordination*. From the point of view of the agents, Thomassen and Lorenzen [THO 01] see coordination as synchronization between the actions of the agents who undertake different activities, reducing the costs of the division of labor as far as possible. From the point of view of the whole system, Rose *et al.* [ROS 02] define coordination as the set of rules and procedures which ensure the functioning of a group.

Coordination is necessary for cooperation. However, if the members of a group are not able to coordinate between themselves, we then speak more of collaboration than cooperation. Coordination implies:

– possession of a distribution function and control of assignment of tasks: point of view of the whole system;

– that it forms an integral part of cooperation and of communication.

Thus, we have just seen that coordination and collaboration are complementary for a cooperative activity.

What kind of cooperation is present in a decision-making process? We saw at the start of this section that Erschler sees cooperation as a renegotiation of constraints between different decision centers. We can mention one school of thought, which stems from management sciences, that defines interaction between managers as being based on conflict rather than on collaboration (see [EAS 91], and [BRU 89]). In terms of decision-making, cooperation can be seen as a negotiation between different agents where the process of discussion becomes essential. As regards decision-making, the dimension of negotiation forms an integral part of cooperation. We propose to define different types of cooperation, integrating the notion of negotiation. This is the object of the next section.

According to Winer [WIN 94], there is a difference between cooperation, collaboration and coordination based on learning activities and examples of collaborative situations in the field of education.

Cooperation: is an informal and short-term relation, without a clearly defined goal, where each cooperator looks for the information which he/she is interested in. The information is only shared if need be. Each organization retains its own separate authority, resources and rewards; there is no danger in working together.

Coordination: is a more formal relation, which requires planning and division of the roles of all the players. It opens channels of communication between the organizations involved. The authority remains within each individual structure, even if risk-taking increases, with a possibility of a problem in terms of distribution of power and influence. The resources are available for all participants to use, and the rewards are mutually recognized.

Collaboration: is a more long-lasting and interesting relation. It is clearly defined and is supposed to be mutually beneficial for the organizations involved, who can achieve common goals. The respective organizations of the participants unite in a new structure, with complete commitment to the common goal. This type of group relation involves effective planning and well-defined communication channels at all levels of the organization. It is the collaborative structure which is formed that determines where authority lies. The risk incurred is greater, because all the participants pool their resources and stake their reputation for the proper function of the collaborative structure. Similarly, the results and rewards are shared. The notion of power and hierarchical progression may therefore pose a problem, because the distribution of power between the organizations to which the participants belong may be unequal.

This analysis to be found in Séguy [SÉG 08] is of course adapted to the context of education.

Yet whatever the definitions of the concepts of collaboration, cooperation and coordination stemming from the different disciplines, there are different forms of cooperation.

3.2. Types of cooperation

What we propose is to define different types of cooperation, established depending on the different interactions possible between the user and the system: complementary cooperation, interdependent cooperation and finally negotiated cooperation.

3.2.1. *Complementary cooperation*

Each agent, artificial or otherwise, has a clearly defined task to perform, depending on its capacities and/or the context (organization) in which it is situated. The assignment of a task to one or other of the agents is changeable. It may be fixed at the outset by the designer of the system or be configured to evolve as the task is done. The main characteristic of this type of cooperation relates to the fact that there is no interference between the tasks: they are genuinely independent of one another. Thus, each task has a very precise and standardized qualification.

In this case, the general objective is not necessarily shared or even known by all those involved. Rather, the emphasis is placed on the notion of the tasks needing to be performed. It is in accordance with these tasks, and the skills of each partner, that the agents' roles are attributed.

3.2.2. *Interdependent cooperation*

Each partner acts dynamically depending on the task that he/she choose to carry out. As with complementary cooperation, the roles are neither static nor decided upon in advance, but depend on the request or the response of each partner. Rather, there is a consensus about the allocation of the tasks or an opportunistic intervention. In this case, the goal must be known and shared by all the partners. From the point of view of organization science, this type of cooperation is comparable to mutual adjustment, where each of the actors finds their place in the organization based on the position of the others, and on the exchanges between all of them [MIN 79]. Other writers define it as integrated cooperation (Schmidt [SCH 91]).

3.2.3. *Negotiated cooperation*

Each partner has a position to defend or negotiate, which is – to a greater or lesser extent – in competition with those of the others. There is no previous agreement or *entente* between the different partners. The approach of this type of cooperation relies on discussion between the different interested parties. Reasoning and its progression, along with explanations (in the broad sense of the term) play a dominant role here. In this case, each partner pursues his/her own objective, which he/she may hide from the others or even deliberately disguise. This type of cooperation has also been defined by [SCH 91] as contradictory cooperation.

The three types of cooperation which we have defined enable us to best specify the roles of each partner in a process of interaction, be it in a cooperative approach or for decision support systems. These three types of cooperation enable us to better define, in terms of human/system interaction, the way in which the users will interfere with the system.

Looking at this man/machine relation, we specify the system for the designer. In this sense, we increase the quality and efficiency of the man/machine pair.

We have also defined a hierarchy in the degree of cooperation, from the least cooperative – complementary cooperation – to the most cooperative – negotiated cooperation. Furthermore, we have also defined cooperation as a continuous scale of cooperation, where the "degree zero" of cooperation would be a very static distribution of the roles and tasks, and thus complementary cooperation (see Rosenthal-Sabroux and Zaraté [ROS 95]).

The notion of cooperation is a very broad concept, which can be applied both to an extensive company and to inter-organization cooperation, or more simply applied to several individuals, and to the notion of decision-making, giving us the notion of collaborative decision-making, which will be presented in the next chapter.

4

Cooperative Decision-Making

A school of research has been formed around *cooperative decision-making*, an emerging concept. The majority of the work done in relation to collaborative decision-making has its roots in the field of computing.

Based in the domain of computer supported collaborative work (CSCW), Karacapilidis [KAR 01] associates collaborative decision-making with an argumentative process where each participant has to consider the other participants to understand the constraints and the solutions to the problem at hand, and the interests and priorities of each player.

More specifically, for the development of multi-agent systems, for Panzarasa [PAN 01], collaborative decision-making is associated with a group of distributed agents who cooperate to achieve objectives which are beyond the individual capacities of the agents. Other authors apply themselves to developing multi-agent systems for which problem solving – i.e. collective decision-making – will work by interactions between the different agents and the solution emerges gradually (Gleizes [GLE 04]).

For [LAB 06], collective decision-making is defined as a "convergence of cognitive and visual interactions, either planned or opportunistic, where people agree to come together for a common goal: for a definite period of time, either in the same place or in different ones, with the aim of taking decisions".

In the field of development of industrial systems and more particularly the domain of e-maintenance, [SÉG 08] associates collaborative decision-making with a process, expressing a series of intermediary stages leading a group of actors to make a certain decision. She summarizes collaborative decision-making thus:

– not every actor belonging to the group must necessarily be involved in the decision being made; he/she may simply contribute to a certain stage of the process – e.g. the search for information needed for the decision;

– the level of responsibility or skill of the actors plays an important role in decision-making (e.g. if two maintenance workers perform an intervention, usually, one of them, having a greater measure of responsibility than the other, will ultimately make the decision, even if the second helps him/her in this task by providing the information and knowledge in his/her own possession);

– a collaborative decision is associated with the whole of the process and all those involved in it, leading to the taking of a decision, rather than with a single decisional activity undertaken by a collective (this corresponds to codecision);

– the actors may not necessarily be human: a man/machine collaboration is also possible.

Jankovic [JAN 06] seeks to support the process of collaborative decision-making using an approach taken from project management. For her, collaborative decision-making is to be viewed as a complex phenomenon for various reasons:

– in collaborative decision-making, the participants have different objectives, knowledge and views as regards the problem;

– the objectives of the collaborative decision are different to the objectives of each individual decision-maker, and represent an aggregation of these objectives;

– the criteria used in collaborative decision-making are not homogeneous. Each field where collaborative decision-making operates has its own criteria and relations, as well as influences between the criteria and the objectives. These influences and relations may not be explicitly known;

– the operational processes that influence, and that are influenced by, collaborative decision-making are interconnected;

– collaborative decision-making depends on the information, on the outputs from the different operational processes, which are ever changing and which therefore introduce a degree of mis-prediction into the decision-making process.

[JAN 06] proposes to view this complex process of collaborative decision-making from four different perspectives:

– the angle of the objectives, whereby the objectives of the collaborative decision represent a goal to be achieved by way of one or more operational processes in the domain of joint responsibility. These objectives may be different from the operational objectives for each process;

- in summary, the different objectives of the collaborative decision, the relations between the different objectives and the actors' preferences are identified at this level;

– the angle of the environment, which is made up of the context of the decision and the actors involved in the decision-making process. Jankovic also defines three factors of influence for the context: the risks of taking the decision, the uncertainty and the importance of the decision in the organization. As regards the actors, she defines three categories of actors: the leader of the collaborative decision, the decision-makers and the contributors;

- the decision, the environments of the project and the organization, the actors participating in these different environments and the different influential groups are identified at this level;

– the angle of the processes, for which she observes that there is no optimal solution: the solution must be negotiated between the collaborators; the process is dependent on having the right information at the right time; the complexity of collaborative decision-making causes problems of coordination as well as assignment of tasks;

   - three global phases of collaborative decision-making are identified: identification of the needs of the collaborative decision, taking of the decision and then implementation and evaluation;

– the view of the transformations, which involves preparing the transformations resulting from the collaborative decision, implementing these transformations and facilitating effective monitoring of the process.

Other writers stress the need for knowledge and for knowledge sharing in order to bring a collaborative decision to fruition. Fu [FU 04] demonstrates the need for knowledge for collaborative decision-making in design processes, while Parsa [PAR 07] offers a Web-based environment enabling knowledge sharing.

A number of other authors define collaborative decision-making as a process.

4.1. Process of collaborative decision-making

Collaborative decision-making is the result of a complex activity involving numerous actors. For certain authors, this activity is expressed by defining a process.

Kvan [KVA 00] breaks down the activity of design into a series of individual or collective stages, considering that the actors work individually on parts of the problem.

Chiu [CHI 02] views the process of collaborative decision-making as a loop in which the cyclical process continues until the objective sought is achieved.

It should be noted that the processes cited above are very specific to the field of design.

It is difficult to generically define a process of collaborative decision-making that is independent of the domain of activity.

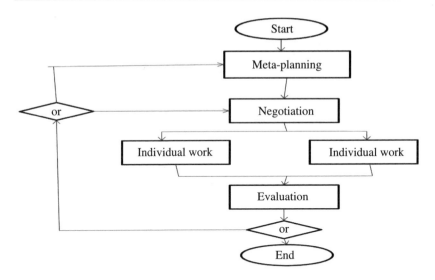

Figure 4.1. *Model of collaborative design [KVA 00]*

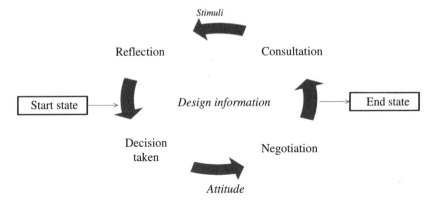

Figure 4.2. *Model of the process of collaborative design [CHI 00]*

We note, however, that collaborative decision-making is a concept which has been gradually emerging over the past few years, which has been the subject of numerous studies in various domains of application such as design, project management, etc.

We propose a model of collaborative decision-making based on a project published in the area of project management.

4.2. Model of the process of collaborative decision-making

To describe the process of collaborative decision-making, we propose a model including all the dimensions and angles put forward in the project management-oriented analysis in [JAN 06]. The process of collaborative decision-making is viewed as a project which needs to be managed, considering all the actors involved and their various objectives. We have used the Unified Modeling Language UML 2.0 to build this model – a generic model which takes account of all the dimensions of the process of collaborative decision-making. Depending on the different systems to be developed, this model will be implemented to a greater or lesser extent, and may be partly expanded upon.

This model is described in the form of a class diagram, and shown in Figure 4.3. In this figure, we have set apart the information relating to the different angles: objectives, processes and transformations. The environmental angle is not represented here, because it relates to knowledge of the product being manufactured, which is very specific to [JAN 06]. In this view, we are interested in the institution's know-how as regards the organization of the project but also the channels of communication and processes of decision-making specific to the organization. An abstract concept such as know-how is difficult to represent in the form of a modeling language such as UML. It would be interesting to consider other modeling languages which are able to model skills and knowledge. However, we believe it is possible – and necessary – to model this know-how in knowledge-based systems, e.g. in the form of production rules, which would help in the collaborative decision-making process.

The perspectives of the objectives offers an overall view of the objectives of the process of collaborative decision-making and of the relations between these objectives. We believe collaborative decisions are decisions for which the actors have different operational objectives. Hence, the class "Actor" is associated with the class

"Objective". An actor may have one or more objectives, and an objective may be held by several actors. Each actor will have a role to play in the process of collaborative decision-making, so the class "Actor" is linked with the class "Role".

The class "Collaborative_Decision_Objective" represents a class of aggregation of several "Operational_Objective" classes. These classes are defined by their names (Decision_Obj_Name), their values (Defined_Value) and the deadline for their realization (Objective_Milestone) so that the project is not delayed. The class "Collaborative_Decision_Objective" also has a link with the class "Client", which may not necessarily be present in every collaborative decision-making process. The attribute "Enterprise_Goal" is a class of association between "Collaborative_Decision_Objective" and "Client". The class "Actor" inherits from the class "Client", as clients influence the decision-making process.

The class "Collaborative_Decision_Making_Process" is characterized by the attributes "Name", "Decision_Importance" and "Decision_Making_Phase". This class is made up of the class "Resources", which itself comprises the classes "Material_Resources" and "Human_Resources". The class "Human_Resources" is a generalization of the class "Actor". The class "Actor" has an oriented association with the class "Collaborative_Decision_Making_Process", denoted as "participates in".

The class "Collaborative_Decision_Making_Process" has a class of association with the class "Data" and the class "Plan". The class "Plan" comprises various activities represented in the class "Tasks". The class "Data" is described by several attributes: "Data_Name"; "Data_Responsible" (the person qualified to deliver the information); "Data_Type" – two types are defined, depending on whether the information is used to prepare the decision or for implementation; "Data_Storage" – the place where the information is located (this may be a database or a written document) – and finally "Data_Criticality" – which corresponds to the probability of obtaining the information in time to make the decision. The class "Plan" is characterized by the attributes "Plan_Name", "Plan_Type" – preparatory or implementation plan – "Responsible" (the responsible party) and "Plan_Storage" – an indication of where the plan of action is located. The class "Plan" is a parent class of the class describing the class "Task" ("Task_Type", "Task_Name", "Criticality", "Task_Responsible"). For more detail about this model, see Jankovic and Zaraté; [JAN 11].

This class diagram is shown in Figure 4.3.

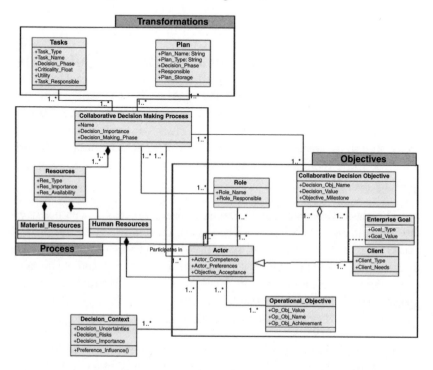

Figure 4.3. *Generic model of the process of collaborative decision-making*

We have defined a new notion: *collaborative decision-making* as a process. This process is described in a very generic manner in Figure 4.3 above. This model can serve as a basis for the implementation of any system, for systems which may integrate all or part of this model.

Having defined this new concept of collaborative decision-making, we now look at systems capable of offering support to these new processes.

5

Activity Support Systems

In this chapter, we define a number of systems capable of offering support for human activity, and specifically to decision-making.

To begin with, we offer a brief history of decision support systems (DSSs), tracing their progression from their initial definition to the emergence of intelligent IDSSs. We also show their evolution toward business intelligence and group decision support systems (GDSSs).

5.1. Interactive decision support systems

The concept of decision support systems (DSSs) emerged in the early 1970s. One of the very first authors to introduce and promulgate this concept was Scott Morton [SCO 71], who introduced the notion of management decision systems. His book, on decision and management, was based on research involving computers, analytical models and terminals using visualization and interactive techniques. This approach is based on analysis of the key decisions, and offers decision-makers a support, an aid to their process of decision-making. This aid is necessary in complex and poorly structured situations, and can be used by decision-makers alongside their own intuitive judgment of the problem and its solution.

One of the most commonly cited definitions is that of Keen and Scott Morton [KEE 78, p1]. DSSs involve the use of computers to:

1) assist decision-makers in their process of decision-making in semi-structured tasks;

2) aid rather than replace the judgment of the decision-makers;

3) improve the quality of the decision-making rather than the efficiency.

Many other definitions have been published which refer to this definition, with certain adjustments.

Keen and Scott Morton first explain that this aid is given by machines, and then specify the context in which it may be given. Finally, in two more points, a very important distinction is drawn between efficiency and effectiveness.

The adjective "efficient", corresponding to the term "efficiency", implies a response to a given task that is as good as possible in terms of a number of performance criteria, whereas the adjective "effective", corresponding to the term "effectiveness", implies identifying what needs to be done and ensuring that the criteria chosen are relevant. The term "effective" requires adaptation and learning with the risk of redundancy and false starts, whereas "efficient" implies refocusing of the objective and minimization of time, cost and/or effects required to bring an activity to fruition.

The concept of a decision support system is based on a balance between human judgment and processing of the information by the computer. Keen and Scott Morton present DSSs as systems devoted to semi-structured tasks. The criteria for the development of such systems are very different from those for structured situations. The keywords are "learning", "interactivity", "support" and "evolution", rather than "replacement", "solution", "procedure" and "automation".

Sprague and Carlson [SPR 82, p.4] gave a definition very similar to that given by Keen and Scott Morton: DSSs can be characterized as computerized, interactive systems which help decision-makers by using data and models to solve poorly structured problems. Their definition is based on the words "data" and "models", which define the architecture of DSSs put forward by the same authors.

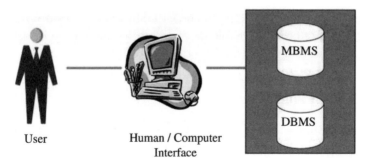

Figure 5.1. *Architecture of DSSs put forward by [SPR 82]*

This architecture is made up of: a human/computer interface; a database management system (DBMS) including the database, and a model-based management system (MBMS) including a model base. The database contains all the data required to solve the problem. In the model base, all the models of the problem to be solved are stored, in order to be able to use the most appropriate model depending on the user or the state of advancement of the process.

Bonczek, Holsapple and Whinston [BON 81] attempted to find common ground between these numerous definitions.

We need only observe that these definitions all suggest that the system must aid the decision-maker in solving un-programmed, poorly structured (or semi-structured) problems.

A review of the definitions also shows that there is a broad consensus as to the fact that the system must have interactive faculties in order to be able to ask questions of the user.

These definitions constitute a brief historical overview of DSSs. The very classical architecture of these systems has, itself, evolved to give rise to other types of decision support systems, which will be presented later on in this chapter. Because DSSs include a database and associated DBMS, the users of these systems find themselves dealing with large quantities of data. Indeed, during the 1990s, for organizations storing masses of information, the use of the right piece of data for the right decision-maker at the right time became a very important problem. The DBMS part of DSSs evolved toward business intelligence in order to enable users with little knowledge of database command languages to find the right data at the right time.

5.2. Business intelligence

One definition of business computing could be: a decision support tool, based on a database bringing together and homogenizing the information from the different departments within an organization. A data warehouse is a very large database which can house several terabytes of data.

The decisional information system is a set of data organized in a specific manner, easily accessible and appropriate for decision-making or an intelligent representation of these data using specialized tools. The aim of a decisional system is to guide the company's actions.

Decisional systems are aimed at the management of the company to help guide its activity, and are indirectly operational because they only rarely offer the means to apply the decisions. They constitute a summary of internal or external data, chosen for their relevance and functional transversality, and are based on particular mass storage structures (data warehouses, on line analytical processing (OLAP) databases). The main advantage to a decisional system is that it offers the decision-maker a cross cutting view of the company, integrating all its dimensions.

A data warehouse enables the decision-maker to work in an informational, referenced, homogeneous and chronological environment. This technique allows users to avoid the problems relating to the heterogeneity of computer systems and of the various definitions of data throughout the company's history.

Decisional applications can then be used to search the data warehouse for and extract partial knowledge of the company's activity in the fields which concern the decision-maker at a given time.

We have also, seen the development of a new concept which combines data warehouses and the Web: the dataweb.

The dataweb contains the idea of access to a universal database no matter what the hosting platform, its location or the data format. It has been recognized for many years that it is essential to have access to the data internal to the company, but also to external data (see e.g. Blandin and Brown [BLA 77] and [MIN 79]) – external data which may be found, for instance, on the Internet. One of the advantages of the dataweb is that it makes it easier to obtain information from outside the company.

The concept of business intelligence and/or a data warehouse touches on decision support by a data-based approach, and particularly at the strategic level of management of the company. However, a global approach to decision support and specifically the development of decision support systems, tackles these developments from two perspectives: data and models of the problem needing to be solved, not only from a strategic point of view but also a tactical and operational management point of view (for further details see Goglin [GOG 01]).

In the 1990s, DSSs were enriched by techniques rooted in AI, particularly the introduction of a knowledge base into the classical architecture of these systems, so as to give the system the capacity for reasoning. This approach is an expert systems type approach, for which the modes of reasoning and the problem to be solved are modeled first and then used on a machine by way of inference engines.

5.3. Intelligent or knowledge-based DSSs

According to [MAR 03] the components of a DSS can usually be classified into five distinct parts:

– a database management system and the associated database: which stores, organizes, sorts and returns the data relevant for a particular context of decision-making;

– a model base management system and the associated model base: which has a similar role to the database management system, except that it organizes, sorts and stores the organization's quantitative models;

– the inference engine and the knowledge base: which performs the tasks relating to recognition of problems and generation of final or intermediary solutions, along with functions relating to the management of the process of problem solving;

– a user interface: which is a key element in the functions of the overall system;

– a user: who forms an integral part of the process of problem solving.

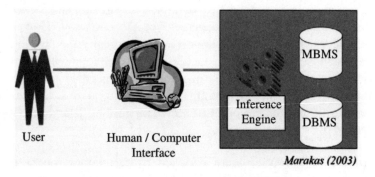

Figure 5.2. *Architecture of DSSs according to [MAR 03]*

Thus, in the architecture of these systems, we see the emergence of a technological part drawn from AI, integrating knowledge modeling into the problem to be solved. The advantage to this architecture lies in the emphasis placed on reasoning in the taking of the decision, and supported by tools such as knowledge-based systems.

Forgionne *et al.* [FOR 02] suggest a conceptual architecture for the next generation of DSSs in the Internet age. Indeed, they propose an architecture for intelligent decision-making support systems (IDMSSs) capable of supporting all the phases in the process of decision-making in a continuous, integrated and complete fashion (see Figure 5.3). The main advantage to this definition is that it places emphasis on the decision-making process. Indeed, the authors suggest different types of support for the different stages of the process. These authors put forward a generic framework that can be used to structure the decision-making process, but do not offer software tools capable of supporting decision-makers, either at each stage or more generally. The overall process is broken down into stages, and each of these stages is fed by data from the database, the model base and the knowledge base. At each stage of the decision-making process, a certain number of elements are expected – the outputs: the report, the parameters and predictions of output, the recommended actions and the explanations and output opinions. This very prescriptive layout offers decision-makers the possibility to take a decision together in a synchronous and non-distributed fashion.

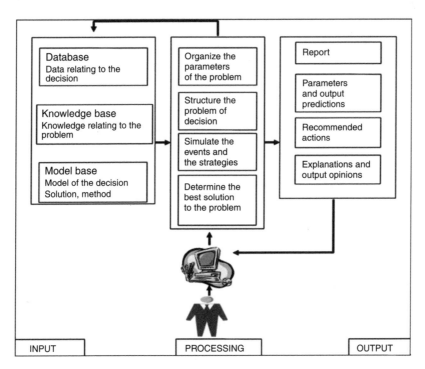

Figure 5.3. *Conceptual architecture for I-DMSSs put forward by [FOR 02]*

An evolution of the architecture, proposed by [SPR 82] is to be able to integrate a knowledge-based system into each of the modules:

– integration of a knowledge-based system into the database, which enables us to get rid of obsolete data and update the data which have been recently used;

– integration of a knowledge-based system into the model base, which enables us to update the models used, and to change them in light of the decisions taken by the decision-maker(s);

– integration of a knowledge-based system into the user interface, which enables us to guide the user in his/her problem solving. This type of system first involves modeling of the user's activity. This model is then used in a reasoning system – in the form of production rules, for instance – in order to guide a novice user in his/her search for a satisfactory solution.

This link between the user interface and the knowledge-based system was made as part of a decision support system for planning rest breaks in a major airline (for further details, see [ZAR 91a and ZAR 91b]).

The advantage of these different links between types of systems is that we can offer support depending on the type of reasoning involved in the decision: data-oriented reasoning, model-oriented reasoning or interface-oriented reasoning.

In knowledge-based systems, a number of authors have defined new types of cooperation-oriented systems: cooperative knowledge-based systems.

5.4. Cooperative knowledge-based systems

As seen in the previous sections, DSSs have evolved to be able to integrate the decision-maker's reasoning. We have witnessed the development of intelligent or knowledge-based DSSs. Knowledge-based systems, for their part, have also evolved, and we have seen cooperative knowledge-based systems appear in the literature.

Soubie [SOU 96] proposes an elementary architecture for a cooperative knowledge-based system. This elementary architecture involves a physical and logical division into three entities: the application part, the cooperation control part and finally the human/ computer interface part.

In Soubie's view, the knowledge base, associated with the inference engine, must be adapted to its mode of representation of the knowledge, and constitutes the artificial agent in cooperative problem solving. Its structure is identical to that of the conceptual model, of the task to be performed in cooperation.

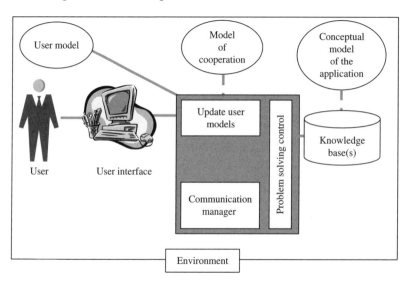

Figure 5.4. *Elementary architecture for a cooperative knowledge-based system put forward by [SOU 96]*

The interface, as a communication tool, is a means of signaling intentional and attentional states, beyond mere transmission of data, by way of the communication acts it enables us to perform.

The cooperation management module is composed of several elements, representing various functions that the module has to perform during and between the cooperative problem solving sessions.

The essential function is the control of the application, but the other two modules are important to ensure the system works properly in cooperative situations.

The application controller performs two functions: implementation of the cooperation strategy, and assignment of sub-problems to the knowledge base.

The communication manager is the intelligent part of the system, intended to provide the system with information about the user's intentions and about the planning of the problem solving, thanks to communication acts performed by the user.

The user update module is used to maintain the pertinence of the system as a cooperative agent.

We can see in this architecture an important fact from a software engineering point of view: the environment is an integral part of the system being designed. In our approach, this environment is comparable to the context in which the decision-maker changes. This fact of taking the environment into account when designing the architecture will more likely give rise to a methodological approach to design that to an entirely separate software module.

This architecture should be compared with the architecture of IDSSs proposed by [MAR 03]. Indeed, we can see a certain similarity. In both cases, the user is seen to form an integral part of the system, or more specifically, of the process of problem solving, the human/computer interface and the communication management system.

In addition, the database and the database management system in Marakas constitute the knowledge base and the application control in Soubie. Also, the model base from Marakas can be seen in the form of three more specific types of models: the user models, the cooperation model and the conceptual application models in Soubie.

Furthermore, Marakas' model management system can be seen in Soubie's module for updating the user models. Marakas' knowledge engine is absent from the setup put forward by Soubie, but he describes his architecture by integrating an inference engine which is necessary for any knowledge-based system. However, we notice two additional elements in Soubie's model: the cooperation manager, including the application controller, and the communication manager. Thus, the division of the modules is not organized in the same way in the two architectures, but the essential elements can be seen in both of them.

These cooperative knowledge-based systems represent a crucial anchoring point for the development of cooperative DSSs.

Indeed, they have all the characteristics necessary to support decision-makers in an asynchronous, distributed situation. Interactive planning of cooperation and of the tasks to be carried out is an essential point, enabling us to structure the process of a group decision in an asynchronous and distributed situation.

Other systems have been developed to support group decision-making.

5.5. Group Decision Support Systems (GDSSs)

Various types of work has been undertaken to improve the function and performance of groups in solving a decision-making problem. According to Jabeur and Martel [JAB 05], we can distinguish three perspectives of work:

– a structural perspective: projects carried out from this perspective focus essentially on the structures and functioning rules of small groups;

– a mathematical perspective: projects carried out from this perspective focus on the problems relating to the aggregation of individual preferences with a view to establishing a collective preference or consensus;

– a technological perspective: projects carried out from this perspective focus on the contributions of ICT to support group decision-making.

Belonging to the technological perspective, there are group decision support systems: GDSSs. These systems arose from an American school of thought. The vanguard in the development of these systems – G. DeSanctis, R. Gallupe., M. Vogel and J. Nunamaker – all work at the University of Arizona, and developed a group decision support system. Let us also point out a European train of thought, led by Liam Bannon [BAN 97], where the approach has its roots in the computer supported collaborative work (CSCW) movement. These systems use communication infrastructures alongside quantitative and heuristic decision support models. These systems were initially installed in a room dedicated to the use of GDSS. This type of room requires physical organization of the computers. The characteristics of such a room are as follows:

– each participant works on a computer;

– a facilitator (leader) coordinates the system use session;

– the room contains a large screen which all the users can see;

– the computers are networked and use a client/server architecture;

– a session of use of the system is generally organized as follows (in accordance with a technique known as DELPHI):

- online brainstorming (discussion forum);

- organization of the different ideas on the main screen by the leader;

- sorting of the different items;

- individual votes about the decisions to be taken, followed by aggregation of the votes by the computer program;

- automatic report on the use session.

This system can be used in synchronous, non distributed mode in the decision room dedicated to that purpose. Such systems can also be used in asynchronous distributed mode over the Internet (for further details on these systems, see DeSanctis and Gallupe [DES 87]).

Let us also cite a particular system, developed by T. Bui, University of Hawaii: the CooP system. It offers the same functionalities as those described above. It exhibits the advantage of being freely accessible and easy to install (see [BUI 87]).

The essential limitation of these types of tools for collective decision-making lies in the lack of dynamism. The tasks and roles are not assigned dynamically. The main advantage to this type of tool lies in the aggregation of the different decision-makers' various preferences and especially in the voting support and the possibility of having each member of the group participate anonymously (or otherwise).

One of the strategically advantageous aspects of computer systems in companies is that they can support decision-making by interactive decision support systems. The extension of organizations to their partners, amongst other phenomena, contributes to an evolution in decision-making. Decision-makers are involved in a global decision-making process without necessarily having proper mastery of that process. We therefore see greater autonomy of these particular actors within the company, and see their responsibilities become increasingly diffuse and increasingly interlinked. Group decision support systems must therefore integrate use constraints such as the impossibility of there being spatial or temporal unity between all the decision-makers involved in a process. Thus, the situation is one of asynchronous and distributed decision-making.

However, the use of group decision support systems requires the introduction of an additional actor: the facilitator or session leader.

5.6. Facilitation of group decision-making

GDSSs stem from collaborative technologies and are very widely used, and have improved participation of the users and the quality of the decision. They were developed so as to provide a computational aid in collaborative decision-making processes ([DES 87]).

In addition, the facilitation activities must accompany such a process, and it is then greatly advantageous to work with a facilitator.

From the point of view of virtual organizations, the facilitators are in crucial positions because they have to control the efficiency, quality and commitment of the solutions, but also make a report to the organization.

From this point of view, the facilitator is the most important element of GDSSs (Nunamaker *et al.* [NUN 97]). A GDSS cannot work in areas such as the functioning of the group and management of non-verbal communications, or organization of a group decision session. These facilitation activities can only be done by human beings. Conversely, the combination of effective facilitation support tools with human facilitation activities can lead to more effective decision-making meetings. An important question then arises: how are we to plan and coordinate between the members of a group using a GDSS?

With the latest developments in GDSSs, many facilitation tasks can be automated – or at least partially automated – so as to improve group communication and the capacity of the facilitator to control the meeting processes. An effective system would reduce the need to develop technical skills. Thus, an automated process to help even a very inexperienced facilitator should include tools to help control the group and the behavior in individuals: indicators which suggest when to introduce pieces of information and when to use particular techniques which could encourage the group to converge toward a consensus.

Facilitation of a group is defined as a process during which a person, to whom all the members of the group are amenable, intervenes to help improve the way in which the group identifies and solves problems and makes decisions (see [SCH 94]). Facilitation is a dynamic process which involves managing the relations between the people, the tasks, the technology, but also structuring the tasks and contributing to actually accomplishing the results which need to come from the meeting.

Another viewpoint is that of Ackermann and Eden [ACK 94], who consider facilitation as an aid for groups to freely contribute to the debate, concentrate on the task, serve the interests of all the players and increase motivation to solve the problem, evaluate the progress made and deal with complicated issues rather than skirting around them.

Another task of facilitation is to engage the group in creativity and in techniques to formulate the problem, helping the group to reach solutions to the issues they face (see [FRE 07]). Facilitators are present in the process of decision-making while the decision-makers are concentrating on the questions relating to the decision.

There may be different forms of facilitation of group decisions.

Human facilitation has been identified as a set of activities which the facilitator has to perform before, during and after the meeting, in order to help the group throughout the decision-making process (see Bostrom *et al.* [BOS 93]). This is one of the keystones of the successful use of GDSSs. A number of studies have shown that the performance of a group is improved when the individuals take part in facilitated discussions and when they can have cognitive feedback (see Reagan-Cirincione [REA 94]).

Automated facilitation is the enrichment of a GDSS with responses, which guides the decision-makers in structuring and executing the decision-making process (see Limayem and DeSanctis [LIM 00]).

According to [NUN 97], electronic facilitation must be able to perform four functions:

1) provide technical support at the beginning and end of the run time of specific software tools;

2) supervise the meeting, maintaining and updating of the agenda;

3) help plan the agenda, and finally;

4) provide organizational continuity and rules for implementing the decision and maintaining an organizational warehouse of the decisions taken.

According to [SCH 94], a more complex function to carry out is improving the group's future performances, which requires the facilitator to "lead the group to concentrate on a specific problem, but also and at the same time on the process of decision-making".

However, for De Vreede *et al.* [DEV 02], a distinction must be drawn between technical facilitation and facilitation of the group's process.

For Kolfschoten *et al.* [KOL 06], technical facilitation is aimed at helping the participants use the technology, and is often done by a chauffeur[1]. The chauffeur's interventions are limited to technical manipulation, but do not relate to the process itself. This kind of facilitation avoids adding communications, and is intended to help the group work. The users must be trained to use the functions of the group system in order to deal with the non user-friendliness of certain programs. Facilitation of a group decision-making process enables us to moderate the participants and their interactions for the tasks described above or, in emergence, to create the results in the meeting. This helps to motivate and guide users in behavioral and procedural problems in distributed environments for which it is difficult to visualize for the users and of their interactions. It also helps manage the transition between the phases for which the participation of the users is crucial for a productive meeting.

Miranda and Bostrom [MIR 99] have another view of facilitation: they consider the tasks relating to facilitation of a meeting from two perspectives: as a process or based on the content. If facilitation is viewed as a process, it is defined as being a set of procedural structures and general support is provided to the group during the meeting. Facilitation seen as a process concentrates the support based on structuring of the tasks, whereas content-based facilitation implies intervention regarding the problem needing to be solved and the decision needing to be taken. This latter type of facilitation thus focuses on the content of the meetings, analysis of the data and revelation of the pertinent issues.

---

1 Translated directly from the author.

This type of activity, facilitation, has led a number of authors to wonder about, and develop, facilitation support tools. These tools were developed using a "collaborative engineering" approach.

5.7. Collaborative engineering

Collaborative engineering is a new field of research aimed at designing and deploying high added-value processes which require collaboration on tasks. The underlying goal is also to design these processes so that they can be easily and successfully used by practitioners without the intervention of professional facilitators (for further details see Briggs *et al.* [BRI 03] and De Vreede *et al.* [DEV 05]). Collaborative engineering includes key roles such as: the *facilitator*, the *practitioner* and the *collaboration engineer*. The facilitator is a professional in collaboration support who designs and leads the collaborative processes so as to support a specific group in attaining specific goals. The collaboration engineer designs and documents the proper practices for the collaborative work and then helps the practitioners implement them. Hence, a process designed by a collaboration engineer has to be transferable and re-usable in order to enable the practitioners to carry it out independently. A practitioner is an expert in the field who learns the practices of a particular task based on a design made by the collaboration engineer. The practitioners do not come up with the processes of collaboration – they only execute them. This reduces the *know-how* that is required, because the practitioners focus on only a part of the collaborative tasks and apply the *know-how* in a particular context of the collaboration process.

These processes are constructed as a sequence of interventions of facilitation which create "patterns" of collaboration known as *ThinkLets*.

These patterns of collaboration can be used to predict a group's behavior as regards a particular objective. A ThinkLet is the very heart of collaboration engineering and is defined as: "the smallest unit of intellectual capital required to create one repeatable, predictable pattern of collaboration" (see [BRI 03]).

ThinkLets are variants on six basic patterns of collaboration, which are:

– diverge: to move from a state of having fewer concepts to a state of having more concepts;

– clarify: to move from having less to more concepts deemed to be shared by the practitioners;

– converge: the opposite of the pattern "Diverge";

– organize: to move from less to more understanding of the relationships among concepts;

– evaluate: to move from less to more understanding of the possible consequences of concepts in relation to the goals needing to be achieved, and

– build consensus: to move from having less to more agreement on courses of action.

The most commonly used ThinkLets are: FreeBrainstorm, LeafHopper, RichRelations, ChauffeurSort, StrawPoll and CrowBar.

The originators of these concepts propose a system for which the patterns of collaboration are implemented: FacilitateExpress.

We believe the use of patterns of collaboration to be interesting for groups who have to perform tasks including collaborative parts, and particularly so for decision-making. However, the use of such patterns of collaboration is limited if a working methodology is not defined.

5.8. Cooperative design approach

We have proposed a cooperative approach for the design of intelligent DSSs or knowledge-based decision support systems, comparing the decision-making process defined by Simon [SIM 77] and the process of knowledge acquisition. We propose that this cooperative approach be used in the knowledge acquisition phase. This approach consists of a process broken down into four stages:

– definition of the actors involved;

– definition of the general goal;

– division of the tasks;

– assignment of the tasks to the different actors.

This approach is based on a definition of cooperation which is presented in Chapter 3. The guiding idea behind these works is to reinforce communication and cooperation between the different actors involved in the design of intelligent DSSs. This is a methodology-oriented approach to design (for further details see Rosenthal-Sabroux and Zaraté [ROS 95]).

However, we believe this approach to design to be applicable and extendable to all tasks which need to be executed by a group engaged in a process of collaboration.

More generally, cooperative systems have been developed in order to support groups involved in tasks requiring a high degree of collaboration.

5.9. Cooperative systems

There are different kinds of cooperative systems depending on the overall objective of the task being performed. Their identifying feature is that they support a group engaged in a process of collaboration.

Cooperative systems usually (but not exclusively) refer to the concept of groupware. Work on this has been carried out in the field of computer supported collaborative work (CSCW). The notion of "groupware" first appeared during the 1980s.

A definition of this notion: groupware denotes the ensemble of technologies and associated working methods which, by way of electronic communication, facilitate information sharing on a digital support for a group engaged in a collaborative and/or cooperative venture.

From a technological point of view, groupware straddles the fence between computing and telecommunications. Indeed, technologies from both domains are used.

From the point of view of an information system, groupware is on the boundary between bureaucracy and transactional computing. In terms of the users, groupware tools belong to the range of tools used by bureaucrats, and use datacenters. Groupware accompanies the evolution of the organization of companies.

Groupware satisfies the demand for quality of services rendered by the company (rapidity, efficiency, etc.). Groupware allows collective work in fairly large groups, distributed both in geographical and organizational terms.

Thus, the term Groupware refers to diverse applications, striving for the same goal: to enable geographically remote users to work together as a team. The teamwork can be consolidated by information sharing or the creation and exchange of computerized data.

Most of the time, it covers functions implemented in the form of various tools:

– messaging (instant or otherwise);

– calendar sharing;

– shared document spaces, organized to a greater or lesser extent;

– information exchange (electronic fora);

– contact management;

– workflow;

– electronic conferencing (videoconferencing, chat, etc.);

– surveying and voting;

– joint editing of documents (revision, the Wiki empire, etc.).

The main supports for groupware tools lie in the following tasks:

– Interpersonal communication thanks to electronic messaging and discussion fora;

– Coordination (time, space, tasks) thanks to shared electronic calendars and project management;

– Collaboration by way of electronic meetings, videoconferences and joint editing of documents;

– Group memory and access to information because of the DBMS for documents;

– Broadcast and collecting of information;

– Automation of administrative processes thanks to workflow tools.

A number of cooperative systems have been developed to support different tasks within group work. The following are but a few of the existing tools: FacilitatePro, Kindling, ThinkTank, Grouputer, WebCouncil, Brightidea, Ideascale, Dilaogr, JamespotPro, BrainReactions, CentralDesktop, MeetingWorks, ExpertChoice.

All these tools have been developed to support certain group tasks. They all possess the functions necessary to support group work in collaborative mode. These tools are analyzed in the next chapter, with a view to identifying which of them could adequately support the process of collaborative group decision-making.

Furthermore, other authors have taken an interest in developing systems to support negotiation between several players. A notable example is the "Negotiation Support System", which is very widely used in auction/bidding systems (for further details on this system see Cellary and Kersten [CEL 04]).

A task including various actors can also be defined as a well-establish process concatenating different sub-tasks. Thus, systems exist to support this type of process: workflow tools.

5.10. Workflow

There are a wide variety of definitions for workflow. Here we shall only cite two – one defining what workflow software packages are, and the other defining the central procedures and pieces in workflow:

– Workflow programs: "A set of proactive programs which can be used to manage working procedures, coordinate workload and resources and supervise the progression of the tasks".

– Procedures: "Any set of tasks executed in parallel or in series by at least two members of a group to achieve a common goal".

However, in the domain of Workflow, there are a certain number of key concepts which must be defined – particularly the various types of workflow.

In Workflow applications, we usually distinguish four categories:

– *Production workflow*, which corresponds to management of the company's basic processes. Procedures do not usually change greatly over time, and the transactions are repetitive. For instance, this might include writing insurance contracts, managing disputes, managing customer complaints, etc.

– *Administrative workflow*, which corresponds to all things paper-pushing, usually based on a messaging infrastructure.

– *Ad hoc workflow* for management of miscellaneous or changeable procedures.

– *Cooperative workflow*, managing procedures which evolve fairly frequently and are linked to a small working group within the company.

In a workflow system, there are traditionally two ways for users to access information:

– either by going to look for it in a shared queue...

This is a database-type request, with a queue being generated as a table to which the different actors in a procedure have access. The advantage to this method of request is the possibility of sharing a set of tasks between a group of users.

Indeed, when a task is assigned to a specific profile, it is not necessarily assigned to a specific person. All the tasks are made available to all the people corresponding to the profile, and thus the workload can best be regulated. The trade-off is that users have to go looking for the list of tasks in order to get it, using an infrastructure specific to the workflow tool. We also have to put strategies in place to refresh the list of tasks, because we cannot constantly be watching the queue.

– ...or by receiving it in their personal inbox.

This is a messaging-type request, because the best way of sending a task to be executed to someone is to notify them of it *via* their messaging services, and therefore in their inbox. Here, we use an existing infrastructure, and a standard mode of communication in relation to the habits of a user. Workflow programs that function on this basis are therefore less cumbersome, and the end user has the impression of going through their tasks in the same way as they go through their email. They do not specifically go looking for the tasks that they have to perform, because they arrive directly to the workstation via the messaging service.

In general, most workflow programs are divided between these two categories. In terms of performances, products based on the messaging infrastructure are far more manageable, and therefore easier to implement, and usually cause less workload on the network because they are integrated into an existing infrastructure. Some such systems use no database at all, and merely provide guidelines, enabling users to connect to existing databases within the company.

Many authors have focused on the notion of workflow, but here let us cite Ellis and Kim [ELL 99], who are pioneers in this field.

This type of tool will lend itself very well to any routine tasks for which automation is possible. However, for a cooperative decision, this type of tool is not at all well adapted, in that an automation of the process of decision-making is by no means feasible in an approach to decision support. Clearly, the notion of a workflow tool, supporting well-structured tasks, is difficult to use for decision support, in that decision support systems are intended for poorly structured tasks or decisions. In workflow-type tools, coordination becomes a central concept.

Conversely, for other types of systems – multi-agent systems – the notion of cooperation is crucial.

5.11. Cooperative multi-agent systems

Multi-agent systems are systems made up of a set of agents, located in a certain environment and interacting according to certain relations. An agent is an entity characterized by the fact that it is, at least partially, autonomous. This may be a process, a robot, a human being, etc.

Gleizes [GLE 04] defines cooperation in a way intrinsic to each agent. Cooperation is the condition and mechanism of control of the emergence of a global function of a multi-agent system.

Internal reconfiguration of the system involves each agent reacting to non-cooperative situations (collected previously, and whose consequences are determined in terms of the agent's behavior). She defines a theory of AMASs (adaptive multi-agent systems), which states that for any functionally adequate system (i.e. which performs the desired function), there is at least one system in which the agents are engaged in cooperative interactions. This means that in order to design a system which satisfies the functional requirements, the social attitudes of the agents which make up that system must be an attitude of cooperation. For this, at all times, an agent analyzes locally whether he/she/it is in cooperative interaction with the others. If this is not the case, we say that the agent is in a non-cooperative situation (NCS). This is in direct contrast with the agent's social attitude, and that agent takes action to rectify the NCS and regain a state which he/she/it deems cooperative. No agent is aware of the global function to be performed – this function "emerges" from the interactions between agents. Reorganization of the agents (decided upon locally) is called cooperative self-organization.

We believe this type of tool is interesting for use in cooperative decision-making. Indeed, it has the necessary characteristics to be able to dynamically support the distribution of roles and tasks between the agents which is defined in the next chapter.

Chapter 6 aims to define systems capable of supporting decision-making in a group of human users in a distributed and asynchronous (or otherwise) environment.

6

Cooperative Decision
Support Systems: CDSSs

In this chapter, we define the tools capable of supporting a group engaged in a collective decision-making process, and in any situation: asynchronous and distributed, synchronous and non-distributed (face-to-face), etc.

6.1. Distributed DSSs

Numerous authors have shown that most decision-making situations which managers have to deal with occur in environments which are dynamic, rapidly changing, distributed and often unpredictable. Hence, new systems have been defined: distributed decision support systems. Shim *et al.* [SHI 02] propose to update the agenda put forward by Keen and called the "forthcoming decade of DSSs" and to extend it from 1997 to 2007. Decision-makers in 2007 were vastly different to what they were in 1980. The levels of technology proposed are improving on a daily basis. The new, technologically-advanced generation of DSS users expects more and more functions from these systems. The technologies of the future for DSSs will be supported by mobile tools, mobile e-services and wireless protocols such as Wireless Applications Protocol (WAP), Wireless Markup Language (WML) and i-mode, so that access to the information and to the decision support tools is ubiquitous. Better collaborative functions will help facilitate more interactive processes of decision-making.

Gachet [GAC 02] defines a new vision for distributed DSSs. He proposes the following definition: "A distributed DSS is a collection of services and devices which are organized in a dynamic, unpredictable, unstable network of hardware and software entities working cooperatively for a common goal of decision support." This definition is founded on the following six assertions:

– a distributed DSS is not data-oriented (see Business Intelligence);

– in a distributed DSS, two units of data which are not semantically connected can always be stored on different storage devices;

– a distributed DSS must take advantage of the global and distributed architecture of the Internet;

– a distributed DSS must be able to survive on an unreliable network;

– a distributed DSS must favor mobility, and finally

– a distributed DSS must not replace real (face-to-face) meetings, but rather promote and favor them.

This very generic definition offers the advantage of responding to a demand for the evolution of decision support systems in the context which, as described above, is in the full throes of evolution. This generic definition is valid for a great many systems. However, the lack of concrete proposals – i.e. from a software architecture point of view – is clear. In addition, we believe it is essential that the system architectures proposed be able to reflect the social network involved in decision-making: the actors, and the relations between them.

6.2. Proposal of an architecture

We propose a cooperative decision support workshop called cooperative decision support system (CDSS). This software platform is based on the architecture of DSSs put forward by [SPR 82], but is extended to take account of the needs induced by the evolution of decision-making processes. It includes the existing modules in the basic DSS architecture:

– data base management system;

– model base management system, including all the different models of the problem needing to be solved;

– A human/computer interface.

However, this architecture is extended and therefore contains new components:

– an interpersonal communication tool;

– a task management tool;

– a knowledge capitalization tool; and

– a dynamic human/computer interaction tool.

This software workshop is based on the observations laid out above, and can be used in asynchronous and distributed decision-making situations. It is illustrated in Figure 6.1.

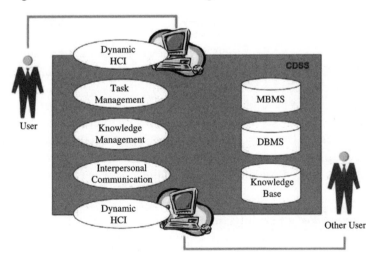

Figure 6.1. *Architecture of CDSSs*

The different modules relating to this platform are detailed in the following sections.

We intend to analyze the type of support which can be provided for cooperative decision-making processes depending on the type of situation in which the actors involved in the process are in. There is a conventional analysis, drawn from the domain of CSCW, of any collective activity in accordance with two criteria: time and space. We then get four types of situations:

– same place, same time (face-to-face);

– same place, different times;

– different places, same time;

– different places, different times.

We suggest using these four situations to classify the types of supports for the particular activity of collective decision support.

	Same time	Different times
Same place	GDSS	
Different places	GDSS Videoconferencing Electronic meeting system Conference calls	CDSS

Table 6.1. *Table of the different situations for collective decision-making*

The situation "same place, different times" is not representative of most cooperative decision-making situations. For this reason, we propose no type of support for this situation.

In addition, as demonstrated in Chapter 2, it is still important for the decision-makers to actually meet. Thus, we also consider that for asynchronous and distributed situations, the process of decision-making must be managed as a project with face-to-face meetings between the different decision-makers and deadlines for the work to be completed.

Thus, the platform we propose comprises several modules. Here we shall only go into detail about the modules added more recently to this architecture: the interpersonal communication tool, the task manager, the knowledge capitalization tool and the dynamic human/computer interaction tool.

6.2.1. *Interpersonal communication tool*

In the decisional processes described above, it seems obvious that the decision-makers should be offered a communication tool. As per the proposal in [GAC 02], it is important to consider that CDSSs have to be supported by an Internet-type infrastructure. Thus, it seems easy to put some form of communication tool in place: messaging, discussion fora, etc.; the crux is to be able to guarantee communication between the different actors involved in the decision-making process.

This type of tool assumes its full meaning in negotiated cooperation as described in Chapter 3. Indeed, in a process of negotiation, it is difficult to envisage breaking the process down into complementary sub-tasks. Also, the main element in the process of decision-making is discussion, and therefore interpersonal communication.

Another module of the platform proposed here is more difficult to implement and requires further research and work.

6.2.2. *Task management tool*

The aim of this tool is to offer solutions or partial solutions to users. It takes care of the division of tasks into sub-tasks and assignment of roles (and therefore tasks) to the actors or agents. This module facilitates cooperation between different users or between the computer and the users. This type of tool comes into its own in complementary and interdependent cooperation as described in Chapter 3. Indeed, this tool must help regulate cooperation and the tasks to be carried out between the different actors involved, monitoring of the tasks which have been completed and re-assignment if necessary. We believe it essential to be able to support cooperation in a group decision-making process. Indeed, the experiment presented in Chapter 2 showed that decision-makers will not naturally make the effort to cooperate in an asynchronous and distributed situation. Therefore, we must be able to help them effectively by assigning them parts of problems to solve and offering them elements of a solution.

The techniques envisaged to ensure the proper function of such a system may be very diverse.

To begin with, here, it makes sense that the systems be similar to the cooperative knowledge-based systems described in Chapter 5. We envisage modeling the decision needing to be taken in the form of tasks and sub-tasks and the associated methods to carry them out. This modeling of the initial problem forms an integral part of the model of the domain offered in the architecture of CKBSs. This modeling is done in the form of a tree diagram of tasks and sub-tasks, which in fact introduces a sequential relation between the different tasks to be performed. This modeling is highly costly and difficult to carry out, for decisions to be taken in an organization, which are generally taken dynamically and often in limited time.

6.2.2.1. *Support for management of non-nominal situations*

This type of aid to task planning has been applied to a support system for management non-nominal situations.

In the structure of the CKBSs, we can see a planning tool which assigns software or human agents to the tasks modeled previously (for further details about this aspect, see Camilleri [CAM 00]). This planning tool has the particularity of being able to manage this assignment of tasks dynamically and, based on monitoring of the various tasks, modify the initial schedule. The advantage to such tools – modeling of the problem in task/method form and the planning tool – is that they offer an interactive and dynamic support for collective problem solving; such interactive and dynamic support is a *condition sine qua non* for decision support. The idea of this project is to provide a decision support for situations in which the context of decision-making is completely atypical. The random aspect in this type of situation is very important. The decisions must be taken beyond the limitations of nominal situations. We define these situations as being non-nominal. Thus, the issue is no longer to find the best possible solution, but rather to find the "least bad" possible solution – i.e. minimize the undesirable effects of the event that has led to this situation. The idea is then to pro-actively support the decision-maker. The system must very quickly calculate the effects of a decision and propose solutions for which the repercussions of critical situations would be reduced. In order to do so, the system has to be able to break the problem down into sub-problems, but must also be able to control the assignment of tasks to agents (human or otherwise).

This project is based on the use of the cooperative knowledge based systems architecture defined by [SOU 96]. This architecture relies on a task/method-type solution paradigm. This paradigm is based on a simple principle of breaking down the objective into sub-tasks with at least one method to deal with each task. The terminal nodes of the breakdown represent the last sub-tasks to be performed.

The problem to be solved will be modeled as follows:

Name: Name of the task

Par: List of the parameters of the task

Objective: Objective of the task

Methods: List of methods that can be used to perform the task

. Our project is illustrated with an example of airplane piloting. In this case, the task to be performed is to transport passengers by plane from one airport to another:

Name: transport_people_by_plane

Par: start: starting point, dest: destination point, ac: aircraft, p: passenger_set

Objective: at(p,dest)

Methods: usual_transport_people_by_plane

For each method, we propose the following form of modeling:

Name: Name of the method

Heading: Task performed by that method

App-cond: Applicability conditions

Prec.: Preconditions needing to be satisfied

Effects: Effects caused by application of the method

Control: Order of control of the sub-tasks

Sub-tasks: Set of sub-tasks

For the example cited above, we get the following model:

Name: usual_transport_people_by_plane

Heading: transport_people_by_plane

App-cond.: start ≠ dest, airport_at(start), airport_at(dest)

Prec.:

Effects: fuel_consumption, at(p, dest)

Sub-tasks: takeoff, cruising, landing

The main model of the task is called the GFM (good functioning model). It can be represented by a hierarchical breakdown of the tasks and sub-tasks. Also, if degraded situations are common, we propose to model them in a different framework: the DTL (degraded tasks library) in order to use them instead of the nominal tasks. This latter model (DTL) and its tasks will only be used when a critical situation arises. Such situations are defined by the lack of applicability conditions of a task from the GFM.

In an operational context, a plan is calculated for a primary task. When an incident occurs, a new plan is calculated which takes account of the collateral effects of the tasks which need to be minimized. Thus, the decision support that the system provides the user with consists of a proposal of a solution for which the collateral effects have been minimized.

In the example cited above, for an airplane piloting task, if an incident occurs during the task of lowering the landing gear, as we have shown, the system can offer the pilot a new plan and thus a decision support, suggesting he/she circle the airport so as to use up all the fuel, in order to minimize the risk of a catastrophic explosion when the plane comes down with no landing gear. The essential contribution of this application is that it offers an approach to re-plan for emergency situations whilst attempting to minimize the undesirable effects of certain tasks. This is an example of interactive planning resolved by an artificial intelligence approach (for further details, see Camilleri *et al.* [CAM 05]).

The major issue with this type of technique is the modeling of the problem. A very fine model must be created even before the system begins to be developed. Also, this type of modeling involves studying the entirety of the environment in which the system is intended to operate before beginning to develop it.

Thus, we envisage other kinds of techniques in order to be able to plan the tasks to be performed in a global decision-making process. Indeed, classic tools drawn from operations research – particularly in optimization – can also be used in this case. For instance, we envisage modeling the problem to be solved in the form of a constrained linear program and using a known solver algorithm. This kind of approach was tested in the project to develop a planning support tool in the context of distance learning.

6.2.2.2. *Planning support tool in the context of distance learning*

The primary goal of this project is to implement and evaluate DSSs for planning distance learning courses. It consists of developing specific DSSs to help teachers in planning distance courses. The project developed two architectures of DSSs in a multi-user context:

– a specific client/server implementation;

– an implementation of a distributed cooperative workshop: CDSS.

The aim of this parallel development was to observe, evaluate, document and bring to bear constructive and positive feedback on that comparison during the different phases of implementation of both

DSSs: the client/server model and the distributed cooperative workshop. These observations focus on evaluating the prototypes' performances, their effectiveness in terms of quality of decision-making, their response times for the scenarios studied and, amongst other observations, their user-friendliness. The project aimed to evaluate the two prototypes from the point of view of their end users – i.e. the teachers and students.

This project included the following phases:

– development of the client/serve DSS;

– development of the CDSS workshop;

– definition of the validation scenarios;

– evaluation of the prototypes developed in the previous phases based on the scenarios defined.

The first three stages were carried out in parallel. For the third stage, an evaluation scenario was defined. This scenario consisted of using a database management system to plan a course for first-year computing students in the context of distance learning. The course is divided into units of seminars, directed work and practical work. For each unit, we want the system to find the optimal means of communication in view of a number of constraints.

These constraints relate to the concatenation of the different units of formation and define precedence constraints as well as the availability of unit supports such as means of communication. We also make provision for the teachers to state their times of unavailability for certain units, and their preferences.

A solver module is written in LPL (Linear Programming Language). This is a programming language and logical, mathematical and structured modeling language. This language and its solver engine can solve extensive linear or nonlinear mathematical problems. LPL is also a distributed system, able to communicate with remote solvers over the Internet and solve complex models (for further details see [HÜR 99] and [GAC 01]).

The assignment of teachers to dispense units is the result of problem solving using LPL, in view of the teachers' preferences and the constraints defined for each of the classes. The total duration of the course will be the result of a function to be minimized between an upper and lower bound. This is another interactive planning approach, solved this time not by artificial intelligence but rather by operations research tools, and specifically linear programming (for further details regarding the third stage of this project, the definition and solution of a scenario, see [DAR 04]).

6.2.2.3. Conclusion

In general, we believe the planning tool constitutes the main contribution in terms of cooperation management. Human/computer or interpersonal cooperation is only possible if that task management tool is capable of quickly re-planning and re-computing the assignments when the context is altered or the problem evolves. This trial-and-error approach ensures the tool's dynamic nature. The tool comes into its own in situations of complementary and interdependent cooperation, because it works out the best possible assignment of tasks dynamically.

In addition, this tool is complemented by a knowledge capitalization tool in order to keep track of the problem solving already carried out or previous solutions to the problem.

6.2.3. Knowledge capitalization tool

We believe it is essential to be able to capitalize on the knowledge of the decision-makers involved in a process, so that all the players can refer to all this knowledge if they need to. Furthermore, decision-makers involved in distributed and asynchronous decision-making processes can be supported by this tool – e.g. by reusing existing solutions, or even simply recycling parts of solutions established previously. The significance of this tool becomes evident in interdependent and complementary cooperation, where the tasks to be performed can be broken down into different distinct parts. An industrial project has helped in the creation of this knowledge capitalization tool.

This work is part of a project aimed at knowledge capitalization in a large manufacturer of electronic, electric and electromechanical systems, products and modules, in the dashboard electronics department, in a Quality Assurance service. This project aims to systematize an approach to quality by rationalized management of knowledge.

Here, two objectives intersect: an industrial objective – improve the company's approach to quality – and an academic objective – test and adapter a method of knowledge capitalization: the GAMETH method (see [GRU 00]). The whole project was carried out in two main parts. The first involved applying the GAMETH methodology and creating a knowledge capitalization tool called COOL (see [HOU 03]). The tool COOL was then used by the company for a period of six months so as to get user feedback. The second major part of the project consisted of collecting the feedback from the various users on this prototype in order to improve the tool, which enabled us to develop a second tool: RECAP.

This study showed us that in terms of knowledge capitalization, it is advantageous to model pieces of knowledge not as fixed objects by as living, dynamic elements. Indeed, they are shared by different types of actors and are used in different task-oriented processes. Also, the development of these tools showed us that different categories of actors, involved to a greater or lesser extent in the task being performed and in the process of knowledge capitalization, have a part to play in a knowledge capitalization process. We distinguish actors who are closer to the knowledge and are therefore more powerful driving forces in terms of production of knowledge. Thus, we believe it interesting to model pieces of knowledge not as static objects or entities, but as entirely separate processes. This is the object of the next section.

6.2.3.1. *Knowledge capitalization: a process-oriented model*

According to Nonaka and Takeuchi [NON 97], knowledge capitalization is to be seen as a succession of various processes enabling us to go from the state of tacit knowledge to explicit knowledge and vice versa, and from individual to collective knowledge. We note the following processes:

– externalization: this turns tacit knowledge into explicit knowledge;

– combination: this enables us to create new explicit collective knowledge;

– internalization: this turns explicit collective knowledge into tacit collective knowledge;

– socialization: this enables us to create new tacit collective knowledge.

We can also note another school of thought, centered around "cooperative learning", with authors such as Johnson and Johnson [JOH 89], who state that "Learning is seen as a social process or a small group of people working together to maximize each individual's learning whilst satisfying everyone's working objectives."

Certain authors take an extended view of knowledge. One example is Blacker [BLA 95], who suggests that knowledge should be considered as an objective in itself, and as a socially constructed process.

Casselman and Samson [CAS 05] propose to examine knowledge from a more holistic standpoint, comparing knowledge and skills, and also to analyze knowledge from four perspectives:

– validity,

– social aspects,

– time-related aspect,

– heterogeneity.

Given that our objective is to develop systems capable of supporting the actors involved in a problem solving process using knowledge, we shall model knowledge capitalization as a process. In order to do so, we propose to analyze this process from the four different perspectives cited above.

For the temporal dimension of knowledge, we introduce:

– a lifetime, with a beginning and end, for each piece of knowledge;

– a global process, enabling us to enter into and get out of that lifetime;

– two states for the knowledge, in order to introduce the concept of validity of knowledge, which can represent a degree of confidence regarding the shared knowledge:

   - knowledge to be shared,

   - validated knowledge.

As regards the validity of the knowledge, we introduce a particular role among the users of such systems: a knowledge *validator*, who has to vindicate or deny the validity of pieces of information provided by other actors. The person playing this role must, of course, be recognized by all the actors involved as an expert in the task being performed, so as to retain legitimacy.

As regards the social aspect of the knowledge, we introduce four roles, corresponding to different degrees of use of the system. These four roles are defined in accordance with the actors' respective degrees of expertise:

Reader (R): someone who only has the right to view or read the information – usually the most inexpert.

Sharer (S): someone who wishes to share a piece of information with other people but who does not validate it. The sharer puts that information on the system.

Validator (V): a person who is recognized by the others as an expert in the field, who awards a mark of confidence to the pieces of information to be shared. These states of confidence can be expressed in the finished system by different colors.

Administrator (A): the person who has all rights in terms of knowledge capitalization: the right to delete, add, etc. knowledge.

Below, we present a model for this process of knowledge capitalization.

There are two situations in which the administrator can remove knowledge from the database:

A(1): either, after a period of time agreed upon by the members of the project, a piece of information has not been validated by any of the members, which implies that that piece of information no longer has any credibility in comparison to the other data.

A(2): alternatively, a piece of knowledge can no longer exist in the database, because the context has changed or the rules have changed.

In Figure 6.2 we distinguish read-access to the database, denoted by bubbles on the left-hand side of the diagram, from write-access, characterized by solid lines on the right-hand side of the figure. (For further details about this process, see [ZAR 05]).

In order to complete the general platform for cooperative decision support systems, a dynamic human/computer interaction tool is needed.

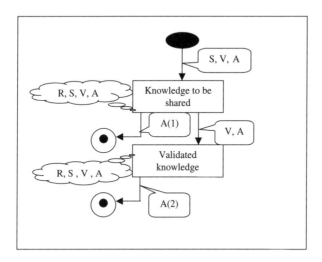

Figure 6.2. *Knowledge capitalization: a process-oriented model*

6.2.4. *Dynamic human/computer interaction tool*

According to Tung Bui, the technologies used to develop DSSs have evolved considerably over the past ten years. If we refer to the architecture of DSSs put forward by [SPR 82], we can see an evolution in the different modules which make up a DSS (see [BUI 02]).

In terms of databases, the entire "Business intelligence" approach has greatly contributed to the evolution of these systems. Many technological advances have been made, reducing the problem of multiple data within organizations or redundant data from different sources.

For model bases, we have shown throughout this book that various technologies contribute to the evolution of DSSs to make them more efficient. Indeed, according to Shim *et al.* [SHI 02], modules based on artificial intelligence have greatly improved the performances of decision support systems.

According to [BUI 02] and [SHI 02] the user interface of DSS remains the area on which researchers and developers should focus their efforts in the future. Indeed, improving the interactivity of these systems will facilitate their evolution.

More generally, for the development of decision support systems, it is necessary to target the responses to the user, in order to be able to provide him/her with the best possible support. Indeed, the right decision for the same problem may be different from one user to another and from one decision-maker to another. Thus, we feel it is necessary to be able to personalize the responses given to a user as much as possible. Hence, being able to take account of user profiles and their evolutions is an important issue in the domain of decision support. Such support systems offer advice to users based on their profile, which represents their preferences as regards a list of valued criteria. The advantage is to be able to provide the user with relevant information. Also, each user will evolve over the course of time and the problem solving process. Hence, the system has to alter the profile of each user as that user evolves and progresses in his/her process of decision. Here, we are talking about counseling systems or recommender systems that integrate profiling or personalization functions. In tools that do integrate user profiles, these profiles are defined for groups of individuals. In the context of system personalization, each user would have his/her own unique profile which would evolve over time. Martin [MAR 12] proposes a method which is able to determine the unique profile of each user, with each user profile being based on numerous attributes. He uses preference aggregation techniques based, in particular, on the Choquet integral and also a learning algorithm such as reinforcement learning.

All these techniques enable us to improve the performances of the tool in question.

Regardless of these proposals for decision support techniques and platforms, it is necessary to define a generic framework for collective decisions.

6.3. Process of group decision-making

Adla [ADL 12] puts forward a generic framework for collective decision-making. He breaks down every process of decision-making into three main phases: pre-decision, decision and post-decision. Similarly, collaborative decision-making processes respect the same pattern with adaptations relating to the group effect. He also proposes a methodology for collaborative decision-making, the original aspect of which is that it provides a framework to help even inexperienced facilitators, and that it offers a two-level architectural model for decision-making: individual and collective. He also describes a state of actions to consider for every facilitator in any decision-making process.

We were able to use this generic framework to analyze a number of tools to support group work in accordance with each proposed phase, and list the possible actions for a facilitator for each tool.

FacilitatePro: This is a Web-based application, published by Facilitate.com in the USA (Facilitate, 1992). FacilitatePro offers supports to send electronic invitations to the participants and to define the problem – i.e. to collect data from previous inquiries and studies, identifying critical issues, discussing and classifying the problems. FacilitatePro also helps to create an agenda. This agenda defines the points around which the taking of the decision hinges. Thus, the participants can access a virtual space where they interact in an asynchronous manner to develop a shared understanding of the agenda. Once the formulation of the problem has been defined and the agenda constructed, FacilitatePro can also be used to present the information to the participants at a later stage. This system enables the user to generate ideas, either anonymously or with their identifying details, if they so desire. The ideas thus generated can be viewed by all the participants, who can use the tool to add comments. The system also offers the possibility to create categories and place ideas into them, organizing them by classes of categories. Furthermore, the tool can be used to organize a vote and have immediate access to the results; there are functions to analyze, summarize and rank these results in hierarchical order.

The results can be displayed in the form of a graph or a table. FacilitatePro also offers functions for elaborating a plan of action with a calendar to monitor a decision, and assigning responsibilities to the different participants; the documentation of the meeting can be generated instantaneously in different formats (Word, HTML, etc.) and can be sent to the participants by e-mail or printed directly; all participants retain free access to the virtual workspace, so that they can monitor progression and prepare future meetings. A simplified, free version of FacilitatePro is FacilitateExpress, which supports the creation of an agenda, generation, categorization and prioritization of ideas, and automatic generation of the minutes.

Kindling: this system is also a Web-based application in this field, which is slightly older and was developed by the Arc90 group (Arc90, 2004) based in the USA. It supports the preparation of the work session by creation of the agenda, invitation of participants and access to the virtual workspace. Kindling allows for generation of ideas in a common space, shared by the participants. It also offers a dedicated space for the generation of ideas, called *rooms*. In these contextual spaces, specific themes of ideas can be classified. This is a way to organize the ideas as soon as they are generated. Kindling offers a "Campaigns" function, specifically designed to support the facilitator of the group, particularly as regards motivating the participants to react to the others' ideas and come up with new ones. The tool also supports the possibility of attributing values to the ideas – e.g. to denote the best among them according to the campaigns. It supports voting, prioritization of the ideas and analysis of the results of the vote. These voting results can be displayed in graph or table from. With Kindling, facilitators can also generate a report of the work accomplished at different levels and by the different users. These documents can be exported in formats such as Excel. The advantage of this tool, like all Web-based environments, is that there is no need for local installation, because the software can be run from the publisher's server remotely. It is therefore sufficient to have a secure connection and a Web browser.

ThinkTank: this system has been one of the most widely used in the domain for several decades, published by GroupSystems (GroupSystems, 1986) based in the USA. ThinkTank offers functions to define the problem by collecting data from previous studies, discussing and classifying the problems. It is also possible to send an electronic invitation to the participants by way of an integral messaging system. The agenda can be drawn up in advance of the meeting with ThinkTank and made available to all the participants, along with other useful information before the meeting. This system offers users a forum to generate ideas. The ideas produced can be seen by all the participants, who can elaborate them or comment on them. ThinkTank facilitates the creation of categories and organization of ideas based on these categories. Voting (binary, decimal, multicriterion, etc.) and prioritization of the ideas are also supported, as are instant production of the results, analysis and summary. The results can be displayed in graph or table form, with calculation of averages and standard deviations. ThinkTank offers functions to create a plan of action with a calendar to monitor the meeting and assign roles to the different participants. A report on the meeting is generated, and can be saved in different file formats (Word, HTML or Excel). The participants can access the virtual workspace for other monitoring activities.

Grouputer: this Web-based system is a solution offered by Grouputer (Grouputer, 1995), based in Australia and launched in 1995. It supports the phases before, during and after the decision-making process. More specifically, it enables users to construct the agenda for the meeting, and thereby define the process which the meeting will follow. Grouputer offers a shared space for generation of ideas, categorization of them, voting on these ideas and prioritization. The tool can also be used to conduct surveys. In the post-decision phase, Grouputer offers the possibility to generate reports, establish a plan of action to monitor the decision and freely access the common virtual space to see how the projects are evolving.

WebCouncil: this Web-based system is a solution offered by CoVision (CoVision, 1985) which, for several decades, has been one of the market leaders in group technology in the USA. WebCouncil covers the pre-decision, decision-making and post-decision phases. It has many sophisticated functions to support a process of collaborative decision-making. Such functions include the agenda builder, a space devoted to the participants' information online and by e-mail invitations. The decision-making phase is also supported by WebCouncil, because it allows brainstorming and commenting on ideas, organization, voting (single choice, classification, scaling and multicriterion voting) and prioritization of ideas. The results can be analyzed and displayed in various forms which facilitate their interpretation (tables and graphs). WebCouncil is also well adapted to monitoring of the decision-making process, because it allows for generation of a report, creation of a plan of action with a calendar and assignment of the tasks to the appropriate parties. Access to the virtual space so as to continue to share information is also possible with WebCouncil.

Brightidea: this system is a product of the company Brightidea (Brightidea, 1999), founded in 1999 and based in the USA. It draws a clear distinction between the different phases of the decision-making process and has appropriate functions to support each of these phases. The pre-decision phase is supported by WebStorm, which helps prepare for the meeting by creating a virtual space and sending e-mail invitations to the participants. WebStorm also supports generation, organization and voting on ideas. Evaluation of the ideas and analysis of the results are performed using the function "Switchboard", which is available in Brightidea. Several methods of evaluation are possible – particularly multicriterion evaluation. These votes can be displayed in graphic or tabular form. The post-decision phase is supported by Pipeline, which offers functionalities to create a plan of action in projects and monitoring of decisions. Brightidea facilitates generation of documents which can be exported in Word format. It presents the advantage of being easily usable because it does not require installation. Users need only have an Internet connection and a Web browser.

IdeaScale: developed by the company IdeaScale (IdeaScale, 2003), this Web-based tool is devoted in particular to collaboration between product developers and their clients in order to better serve the needs and expectations of the customers. Hence, it is not specifically a GDSS, but it enables users to make decisions to improve the quality of the services provided by the product developers and the clients' satisfaction. It supports certain parts of the pre-, during and post-decision phases. In the pre-decision phase, e-mail invitations are sent to the participants, explaining the topic and the goal of the meeting and the URL of the dedicated decision-making space. The participants can go to this address asynchronously for further information. The decision-making phase can be done synchronously or asynchronously, with the participants in the same place or in different places. Ideas can be generated and commented upon in the forum given over for this purpose, and these ideas can also be categorized, voted upon and prioritized. IdeaScale offers analysis of the results, and can display the data in numerical and graphic form. The post-decision phase is supported by IdeaScale because it continues to allow access to the virtual space to consult the activities and their results. It can also e-mail the report to the different participants. Although IdeaScale is free to access, some of its advanced functionalities must be paid for.

Dialogr: this is a Web-based solution for collaborative decision-making, maintained by Dialogr.com (Dialogr, 2007). Free to access, Dialogr is able to support all three phases of the decision-making process. In the pre-decision phase, it allows the user to send e-mail invitations to the various participants, with the URL of the virtual space, and a note explaining the aim of the meeting. The participants can access this space in order to gather information and prepare for the meeting. The actual decision phase is supported by Dialogr, which offers the possibility to generate ideas with comments, evaluate these ideas (award one to five stars to each idea) and prioritize them. The analysis offered is minimal, because it is not possible to perform computations with table and graph displays of the results in order to go into greater depth. Thus, Dialogr is more a decision-making tool for relatively simple problems, for which consensus is not dependent on many factors. A report can be e-mailed to the members of the group at the end of the decision-making phase. users retain the ability to access the space so as to monitor the decision's progress and conduct other useful exchanges.

JamespotPro: This tool is a Web-based application offered by the company Jamespot.com (Jamespot, 2005). It also lends itself to collaborative decision-making in organizations and supports certain stages of the three phases of decision-making that we have defined. In the pre-decision phase, JamespotPro enables the user to define the agenda and invite participants to the session. As regards the decision-making phase, the application supports generation and organization of ideas. In the post-decision phase, it is possible to generate articles from the previous phases and construct a calendar, assigning duties and deadlines for their realization to participants. Similarly, it is possible to have access to the decision-making space to monitor progress.

Campfire: This tool is also a Web-based application devoted to decision-making. It is a solution offered by Campfire (Campfire, 1999), which has been in existence for over ten years and supports certain stages of the process. Campfire supports the pre-decision phase, allowing the facilitator to prepare the decision-making meeting and invite the various parties involved. The decision-making phase is supported by a device for the generation of ideas. It does not have advanced functions to analyze the data, because its essential purpose is to collect and pool ideas. Campfire is able to generate a report and provides access to a forum to monitor the progress of the decision.

BrainReactions: This Web-based application provides basic elements for decision-making. It is a solution provided by BrainReactions (BrainReactions, 2005). This tool supports the following stages in the process of decision-making: preparation for the meeting by creating the decision-making space and sending e-mail invitations to the participants. Generation of ideas is supported by BrainReactions, and it also enables voting on and organization of ideas. There are no functions available for analyzing the results. It is possible to monitor the progress of the decision by accessing the space during the post-decision phase.

CentralDesktop: this system is a Web-based application offered by Central Desktop (Central Desktop, 2005). It mainly supports the pre-decision phase, allowing the facilitator to create the virtual space for the meeting, the agenda and send e-mail invitations to the participants. The decision-making phase is only partially supported, because CentralDesktop only allows for generation of the ideas and categorization of them in accordance with the topics in question. For the post-decision phase, it is possible to e-mail the report and access the decision space for the purposes of monitoring. The advantage, just like with all the other Web-based applications, is that there is no need to install the tool locally, so participants only need an Internet connection and a browser to use CentralDesktop.

Meetingworks: this application is a Web-based solution developed by IBM (Meetingworks, 1994), and which is being used less and less nowadays. However, Meetingworks is a suite of tools which supports all the stages of the different phases of decision-making. It offers a support for creation of the agenda, e-mail invitation and the other stages of the pre-decision phase. One of its devices helps to monitor the evolution of the different stages of the agenda, with real-time display of the execution of the process. Generation, organization and evaluation of ideas are also supported by functions in Meetingworks. Cross-cutting and multicriterion analysis of the results is supported, as is their display in graph and table form. The analysis device offers two levels in the construction of meaning: the individual level and the collective level. Generation and management of the report on the meeting are supported by Meetingworks, as are all the stages of the post-decision phase – particularly monitoring of the decision. This GDSS has other functions which are advantageous for decision-making, such as the timer, document loading, etc.

ExpertChoice: this system is a solution offered by the Expert Choice group (Expertchoice, 1983), founded in 1983. ExpertChoice is a very high-performance tool for decision-making – particularly in the stage of evaluation of ideas using multiple criteria based on the Analytic Hierarchy Process (AHP). However, this tool is not hugely efficient in terms of the phases of data collection, analysis, clarification and paring down of a large number of ideas. The post-decision phase is facilitated by access to the data, generation of the report on the meeting and monitoring of the decision (for further details on this analysis see Konate and Zaraté [KON 10]).

This analysis leads us to the conclusion that the phase of brainstorming in a collective decision-making process is a crucial phase, during which the facilitator would benefit from having help which, in itself, can be implemented in a facilitating support system. Ait-Haddou, Camilleri and Zaraté [AIT 12] propose a tool capable of predicting the number of ideas which will be put forward in a few minutes during a brainstorming session. This tool is based on idea prediction models drawn from the domain of social psychology. These models are mathematically formulated in the form of linear programs and then continuously optimized in order to dynamically find the number of ideas which are likely to surface. This tool enables the facilitator to put a stop to a meeting which is going to become ineffectual.

6.4. Conclusion

The concept of a cooperative decision support system remains a proposition for a software platform. The major principle of this proposition is to be able to offer a globally integrated support to the decision-maker. The main benefit with this type of tool lies in the possibility it offers for a user to solve part of a problem. The system must be capable of reacting dynamically, i.e. reacting based on the users' responses, recalculating and reproposing an assignment of the tasks to the various users. This is made possible by interactive planning of the decisions needing to be taken and/or the tasks needing to be performed.

However, face-to-face contact of the human actors remains an essential element in decision-making. This face-to-face contact is a means for discussion between the different decision-makers.

Thus, we must stress that the use of this type of tool has to be accompanied by a methodology able to manage the global process of cooperative decision-making. Indeed, for strategic decisions which will have a significant financial, human and organizational impact, we believe it is essential to arrange real meetings between the different decision-makers in order to allow them to better negotiate and argue their cases.

General Conclusion

The goal of a designer of decision support systems is to support the decision-making process in an organization as fully as possible. The introduction of ICT into organizations was intended – amongst other objectives – to support the process of decision-making and communication between the actors. We have shown in this book that the support ICT provides for decisional processes is far from ideal, but it does considerably change the decision-making process.

Furthermore, decision-making processes in organizations have evolved, and decision-makers are working more and more in asynchronous and in a distributed mode. The decision support systems offered must thus at the very least ensure synchronization of the actors involved, and at best facilitate genuine cooperation. The help that a DSS can offer involves interactive planning of cooperative tasks.

From an architectural point of view, the architecture initially put forward by Sprague and Carlsson [SPR 82], comprising a database, a model base and an interface, and their respective management systems, has evolved, integrating knowledge-based modules and cooperation management modules. From this point of view, the processes of decision-making in organizations must be supported more by platforms of tools than by specific tools. The main contribution of the platform of tools put forward here, cooperative decision support systems, lies in providing support for cooperative decision-making.

Many decision support systems have been developed, each with different objectives. Some are devoted to a very specific task; others improve cooperation between different decision-makers; others attempt to improve the decision-makers' reasoning models. We believe it essential, in years to come, to improve the human/computer interfaces of such systems. Work on recommendation systems and profiling systems is aimed at improving the responses given to user requests. The integration of this type of work into the realization of CDSSs is highly promising. However, there are many other avenues for research which it would be interesting to explore.

Indeed, the concept of a cooperative interface still has to be improved. For example, in time, this software element must be able to prevent wrong moves by a user which would destroy the progress made by the other users' work.

This function involves using the results from the domain of dialog management and language theory.

From the point of view of the functionalities, we have shown that DSSs are integrating more and more new functions to become cooperative DSSs, which offer management of cooperation between various decision-makers. However, we are fully aware of the limitations of such systems. They are not and make no pretence at being universal; they are definitely not useful in all kinds of group decision processes. Indeed, the role of the facilitator remains a crucial one in group decision-making. Work is currently being done with a view to support the facilitator by automating some of his/her tasks. However, group decision support is easier in a predefined framework in which three stages are defined: pre-decision, decision and post-decision. In spite of the framing of this process, a dynamic tool to support the facilitator remains to be developed.

This type of group decision-making process in an asynchronous and distributed situation will become more and more widespread, due to the increasing use of ambient systems. A new field of research is taking shape: spatial decision support systems, aimed at taking account of the working context of each participant, evolving in mobile mode. It then becomes more difficult to offer activity support.

Another interesting perspective is emerging, centered on the notion of cooperative decision-making for the concept of electronic government, involving citizens in debates in a means of participative democracy. In the existing literature, we define a new group of people – not "Citizens", but "Nitizens: Net citizens". Thus, this is an important issue in terms of development of systems to support decision-making.

Bibliography

[ACK 94] ACKERMANN F., EDEN C., "Issues in computer and non-computer supported GDSSs", *Decision Support Systems*, vol. 12, pp. 381–390, 1994.

[ADL 10] ADLA A., Aide à la Facilitation pour une prise de Décision Collective: Proposition d'un Modèle et d'un Outil, Doctoral Thesis, University of Toulouse, 2010.

[AIT 12] AIT-HADDOU H., CAMILLERI G., ZARATÉ P., "Dynamic models for ideas number prediction in brainstorming", *Hawaii International Conference on Systems Science (HICSS 2012)*, 4–7 January, IEEE Computer Society, Grand Wailea Maui, HI, pp. 382–391, 2012.

[AXE 92] AXELROD R., *Donnant, Donnant*, Odile Jacob, Paris, 1992.

[BAN 97] BANNON L., "Group decision support systems: an analysis and critique", *Proceedings of the European Conference on Information Systems*, Cork, Ireland, vol. 1, pp. 526–539, 1997.

[BLA 95] BLACKER F., "Knowledge, knowledge work and organizations: an overview and interpretation", *Organization Studies*, vol. 16, pp. 1021–1046, 1995.

[BLA 77] BLANDIN J.S., BROWN W.B., "Uncertainty and management search for information", *IEEE Transactions on Engineering Management*, vol. M24, pp. 114–119, 1977.

[BON 81] BONCZEK R., HOLSAPPLE C., WHINSTON A., *Foundations of Decision Support Systems*, Academic Press, New York, 1981.

[BOS 93] BOSTROM R.P., ANSON R., CLAWSON V.K., "Group facilitation and group support systems", in JESSUP L., VALACICH J. (eds), *Group Support Systems: New perspectives,* Macmillan, New York, pp. 146–168, 1993.

[BOU 93] BOURON T., Structure de communication et d'organisation pour la coopération dans un univers multi-agents, Laforia report no. 93/04, February, 1993.

[BRÉ 03a] BRÉZILLON P., "Context dynamic and explanation in contextual graphs", in BLACKBURN P., GHIDINI C., TURNER R.M., GIUNCHIGLIA F. (eds), *Modeling and Using Context (CONTEXT-03)*, LNAI 2680, Springer Verlag, pp. 94–106, 2003.

[BRÉ 03b] BRÉZILLON P., ADAM F., POMEROL J.C., "Supporting complex decision making processes in organizations with collaborative applications – a case study", in FAVELA J., DECOUCHANT D. (eds), *Groupware: Design, Implementation, and Use*, LNCS 2806, Springer Verlag, pp. 261–276, 2003.

[BRÉ 08] BRÉZILLON P., ZARATÉ P., "Group decision making: a context oriented view", *Journal of Decision Systems*, vol. 17, no. 1, pp. 11–26, 2008.

[BRI 03] BRIGGS R., DE VREEDE G., NUNAMAKER J., "Collaboration engineering with thinkLets to pursue sustained success with group support systems", *Journal of Management Information Systems*, vol. 19, no. 4, pp. 31–64, 2003.

[BRU 89] BRUNSSON N., *The Organization of Hypocrisy*, John Wiley & Sons, England, 1989.

[BUI 02] BUI T., "Decision support systems: old problems, new solutions?", IFIP TC8/WG8.3 DSI'Age, Cork, Ireland, 2002.

[BUI 87] BUI T., *A Group Decision Support System for Cooperative Multiple Criteria Group Decision Making*, LNCS, Springer-Verlag, Berlin Heidelberg, Germany, 1987.

[CAM 00] CAMILLERI G., Une approche, basée sur les plans, de la communication dans les systèmes à base de connaissances coopératifs, Doctoral Thesis, University Paul Sabatier, Toulouse, December 2000.

[CAM 05] CAMILLERI G., SOUBIE J.L., ZARATÉ P., "Critical situations for decision making: a support based on a modelling tool", *Group Decision and Negotiation Journal*, vol. 14, no. 2, pp. 159–171, March 2005.

[CAS 05] CASSELMAN R., SAMSON D., "Moving beyond tacit and explicit: four dimensions of knowledge", *Proceedings of the 38th Annual Hawaii International Conference on Science Systems (HICSS'05)*, 3–6 January, IEEE, 2005.

[CAU 05] CAUVIN A., Analyse, modélisation et amélioration de la réactivité des systèmes de décision dans les organisations industrielles, Accreditation to Supervise Research, University Paul Cézanne Aix Marseille III, 2005.

[CEL 04] CELLARY W., KERSTEN G., "Electronic negotiations: models, systems and agents", *Journal of Decision Systems*, vol. 13, no. 4, pp. 371–374, 2004.

[CHI 02] CHIU M.L., "An organizational view of design communication in design collaboration", *Design Studies*, vol. 23, no. 2, pp. 187–210, 2002.

[COU 82] COUBON J.C., "Processus de décision et aide à la décision", *Economies et Société*, vol. 16, no. 12, pp. 1455–1476, 1982.

[DAR 04] DARGAM F., GACHET A., ZARATÉ P., BARNHART T., "DSSs for planning distance education: a case study", in MEREDITH R., SHANKS G., ARNOTT D., CARLSSON S. (eds), *Decision Support in an Uncertain and Complex World*, 1–3 July, Prato, Italy, pp. 169–179, 2004.

[DEL 95] DELAHAYE J.P., "L'altruisme Récompensé?" *Pour La Science*, Paris, 1995.

[DES 87] DESANCTIS G., GALLUPE B., "A foundation for the study of group decision support systems", *Management Science*, vol. 33, no. 12, pp. 1589–1609, 1987.

[DET 96] DE TERSSAC G., MAGGI B., "Autonomie et conception", in de TERSSAC G., FRIEDBERG E. (eds), *Coopération et Conception,* Octaves Edition, 1996.

[DEV 02] DE VREEDE G.J., BOONSTRA J., NIDERMAN F., "What is effective GSS facilitation? Aquality inquiry into participants' perceptions", *Proceedings of HICSS-35*, IEEE Computer Society Press, Hawaii, 2002.

[DEV 05] DE VREEDE G., BRIGGS R., "Collaboration engineering: designing repeatable processes for high-value collaborative tasks", *Proceedings of HICSS-38*, IEEE Computer Society Press, Los Alamitos, 2005.

[DIL 96] DILLENBOURG P., BAKER M., BLAYE M., "The evolution of research on collaborative learning", in SPADA E., REIMAN P. (eds), *Learning in Humans and Machine: Towards an Interdisciplinary Learning Science*, Elsevier, Oxford, pp. 189–211, 1996.

[EAS 91] EASTERBROOK, *CSCW: Co-operation or Conflict*, Springer-Verlag, New York, 1991.

[ELL 99] ELLIS C., KIM K., "A framework and taxonomy for workflow architecture", *Proceedings of the 1999 ACM Conference on Supporting Group Work – GROUP'99*, Phoenix, AZ, November 1999.

[ERS 93] ERSCHLER J., FONTAN G., MERCÉ C., "Approche par Contraintes en planification et ordonnancement de la production", *RAIRO-APII*, vol. 27, no. 6, pp. 669–695, 1993.

[FAL 91] FALZON P., "Distributed decision making: cognitive models for cooperative work", in RASMUSSEN J., BREHMER B., LEPLAT J. (eds), *Distributed Decision Making: Cognitive Models for Cooperative Work*, John Wiley & Sons Ltd, pp. 177–184, 1991.

[FOR 02] FORGIONNE G., MORA M., CERVANTES F., GERLMAN O., "I-DMSS: a conceptual architecture for the next generation of decision making support systems in the internet age", *Proceedings of the International Conference IFIP TC8/WG8.3*, Cork, Ireland, pp. 154–165, 2002.

[FRE 07] FRENCH S., "Web-enabled strategic GDSS, e-democracy and Arrow's theorem: a Bayesian perspective", *Decision Support Systems*, vol. 43, no. 4, pp. 1476–1484, 2007.

[FU 04] Fu Q.Y., Ping C.Y., Helander M.G., "Knowledge-based collaborative decision making system for product design", *IEEE Conference on Cybernetics and Intelligent Systems*, Singapore, 2004.

[GAC 02] Gachet A., "A new vision for distributed decision support systems", *Proceedings of the International Conference IFIP TC8/WG8.3*, Cork, Ireland, pp. 343–352, 2002.

[GAC 01] Gachet A., Hürlimann T., Internet-solver für LPL, Working paper 01-08, University of Fribourg, Fribourg, 2001.

[GLE 04] Gleizes M.P., Vers la résolution de problèmes par émergence, Accreditation to Supervise Research, University Paul Sabatier, Toulouse, December 2004.

[GOG 01] Goglin J.F., *Construction du datawarehouse*, Hermès, 2001.

[GOR 71] Gorry G., Scott Morton M., "A framework for management information systems", *Sloan Management Review*, vol. 13, no. 1, pp. 50–70, 1971.

[GRU 00] Grundstein M., "From capitalizing on company knowledge to knowledge management", in Morey D., Maybury M., Thuraisingham B. (eds), *Knowledge Management, Classic and Contemporary Works*, Chapter 12, The MIT Press, Cambridge, MA, pp. 261–287, 2000.

[HAT 96] Hatchuel A., "Coopération et conception collective", in De Terssac G., Friedberg E. (eds), *Coopération et Conception*, Octaves Edition, 1996.

[HOU 03] Houé R., Zaraté P., Varquez J., Le Lann J.M., "Mise en oeuvre de la méthodologie Gameth pour la capitalisation des connaissances au sein d'une grande organisation", *5ième Congrès Francophone de Génie Industriel GI'03*, 26–29 October, Québec, Canada, 2003.

[HÜR 99] Hürlimann T., Mathematical modeling and optimization: an essay for the design of computer-based modeling tools, Kluwer Academic Publishers, Dordrecht, The Netherlands, 1999.

[JAB 05] Jabeur K., Martel J.M., "La décision de groupe: l'application de méthodes de surclassement de synthèse", *Bulletin du Groupe de Travail Européen Aide Multicritère à la décision*, série 3, no. 11, pp. 1–5, 2005.

[JAN 06] Jankovic M., Prise de Décisions collaboratives dans le processus de conception de nouveaux produits: application à l'automobile, Doctoral Thesis, Ecole Centrale Paris, 2006.

[JAN 11] Jankovic M., Zaraté P., "Discrepancies and analogies in artificial intelligence and engineering design approaches in addressing collaborative decision making", *International Journal of Decision Support System Technology*, vol. 3, no. 2, pp. 1–14, 2011.

[JOH 89] Johnson D., Johnson R., *Cooperation and Competition: Theory and Research*, Interaction Book Company, Edina, MN, 1989.

[KAR 01] KARACAPILIDIS N., PAPADIAS D., "Computer supported argumentation and collaborative decision making: the HERMES system", *Information Systems*, vol. 26, no. 4, pp. 259–277, 2001.

[KAS 93] KAST R., *La théorie de la décision*, La Découverte, Coll Repères, 1993.

[KEE 78] KEEN P., SCOTT MORTON M., *Decision Support Systems: An Organizational Perspective*, Addison-Wesley Publishing Company, 1978.

[KOL 06] KOLFSCHOTEN G., BRIGGS R., DE VREEDE G., JACOBS P., APPELMAN J., "A conceptual foundation of the ThinkLet concept for collaboration engineering", *International Journal of Human-Computer Studies*, vol. 64, no. 7, pp. 611–621, 2006.

[KON 10] KONATE J., ZARATÉ P., Etude Comparative des Systèmes Collaboratifs d'Aide à la Décision: évaluation d'une approche pour la prise de décision collaborative, Research report, IRIT/RR--2010-14--FR, IRIT, 2010.

[KVA 00] KVAN T., "Collaborative design: What is it?", *Automation in Construction*, vol. 9, no. 4, pp. 409–415, 2000.

[LAB 06] LABORIE F., Le concept de salle de décision collective et son application aux processus complexes EADS, Doctoral Thesis, University of Toulouse, 2006.

[LAH 00] LAHLOU S., "Les attracteurs cognitifs et le syndrome du débordement", *Intellectica* 2000/1, no. 30, pp. 75–115, 2000.

[LAV 83] LAVERGNE J.P., *La Décision: Psychologie Et Méthodologie*, Les éditions ESF, Paris, 1983.

[LEM 74] LE MOIGNE J.L., *Les Systèmes De Décision Dans Les Organisations*, Presses Universitaires de France, Paris, 1974.

[LIM 00] LIMAYEM M., DESANCTIS G., "Providing decisional guidance for multicriteria decision making in groups", *Information Systems Research*, vol. 11, no. 4, pp. 386–401, 2000.

[LON 03] LONGUEVILLE B., Capitalisation des processus de décision dans les projets d'innovation : application à l'automobile, Doctoral Thesis, Ecole Centrale Paris, 2003.

[MAR 03] MARAKAS G., *Decision Support Systems in the 21st Century*, 2nd ed., Prentice-Hall, 2003.

[MCG 84] MCGRATH J.E., *Groups: Interaction and Performance*, 1st ed., Prentice-Hall, Englewood Cliffs, NJ, 1984.

[MAR 12] MARTIN A., Evolution de profils Multi-Attributs, par Apprentissage Automatique et Adaptatif dans un système de Recommandation pour l'Aide à la Décision, Doctoral Thesis, University of Toulouse, 2012.

[MEN 03] MENACHOF D., SON B., *The Truth about Collaboration*, Chief Logistics Officer-Penton Media, pp. 6–12, 2003.

[MIL 87] MILLOT P., Coopération homme-machine dans les tâches de supervision des procédés automatisés, Doctoral Thesis, University of Haut Cambresis, Valenciennes, 1987.

[MIN 79] MINTZBERG H., *The Structuring of Organization*, Prentice Hall, 1979.

[MIR 99] MIRANDA S., BOSTROM R., "Meeting facilitation: process versus content interventions", *Journal of Management Information Systems*, vol. 15, no. 4, pp. 89–114, 1999.

[NON 97] NONAKA I., TAKEUCHI H., *The Knowledge-Creation Company*, Oxford Press, 1997.

[NUN 97] NUNAMAKER J., BRIGGS R., MITTLEMAN D., VOGEL D., BAKTHZARD D., "Lessons from a dozen years of group support systems research", *Journal of MIS*, vol. 13, no. 3, pp. 163–207, 1997.

[PAN 02] PANZARASA P., JENINGS N.R., NORMAN T.J., "Formalising collaborative decision making and practical reasoning in multi-agent systems", *Journal of Logic and Computation*, vol. 12, no. 1, pp. 55–117, 2002.

[PAR 07] PARSA S., PARAND F.A., "Cooperative decision making in a knowledge grid environment", *Future Generation Computer Systems*, vol. 23, no. 8, pp. 932–938, 2007.

[PAV 94] PAVARD B., *Systèmes Coopératifs: de la modélisation à la conception*, Octares, 1994.

[POM 04] POMEROL J.C., ADAM F., "Practical decision making – from the legacy of Herbert Simon to decision support systems", in MEREDITH R., SHANKS G., ARNOTT D., CARLSSON S. (eds), *Proceedings of the International Conference IFIP TC8/WG8.3*, Prato, Italy, pp. 647–657, 1–3 July 2004.

[REA 94] REAGAN-CIRINCIONE P. "Improving the accuracy of group facilitation social judgment analysis and information technology", *Organizational Behaviour and Human Decision Processes*, vol. 58, no. 2, pp. 246–270, 1994.

[ROS 02] ROSE B., GARZA L., LOMBARD M., LOSSENT L., RIS G., "Vers un référentiel commun pour les connaissances collaboratives dans l'activité de conception des produits", *Actes du 1er Colloque du groupe de travail Gestion des Compétences et des Connaissances en Génie Industriel du GDR MACS*, pp. 85–90, 2002.

[ROS 96] ROSENTHAL-SABROUX C., Contribution Méthodologique à la conception des Systèmes d'Information Coopératifs: Prise en compte de la coopération homme/machine, Accreditation to Supervise Research, University of Paris Dauphine, France, 1996.

[ROS 98] ROSENTHAL-SABROUX C., ZARATÉ P., "A cooperative approach for intelligent decision support systems", *Proceedings of the International Conference (HICSS'31)*, 6–9 January, Hawaii, 1998.

[ROS 95] ROSENTHAL-SABROUX C., ZARATÉ P., "Cooperation typology for decision support", *Proceedings of the International Conference (COOP'95)*, Antibes, France, pp. 254–265, 25–27 January 1995.

[ROY 85] ROY B., *Méthodologie MultiCritère d'Aide à la Décision*, Economica, Paris, 1985.

[ROY 93] ROY B., BOUYSSOU D., *Aide multicritère d'aide à la décision*, Economica, Paris, 1993.

[SCO 71] SCOTT MORTON M., *Management Decision Systems, Computer Based Support for Decision Making*, Harvard University, Boston, MA, 1971.

[SCH 91] SCHMIDT K., "Cooperative work: a conceptual framework", in RASMUSSEN J., BREHMER B., LEPLAT J. (eds), *Distributed Decision Making: Cognitive Models for Cooperative Work*, John Wiley & Sons Ltd, New York, pp. 75–110, 1991.

[SCH 92] SCHMIDT K., BANNON L., "Taking CSCW seriously", *Computer Supported Cooperative Work (CSCW' 92)*, vol. 1, no. 1, pp. 7–40, 1992.

[SCH 94] SCHWARZ R., *The Skilled Facilitator*, Jossey-Bass Publishers, 1994.

[SÉG 08] SÉGUY A., Décision collaborative dans les systèmes distribués. Application à l'e-maintenance, Doctoral Thesis, University of Toulouse, INPT, Spécialité Systèmes Industriels, 2008.

[SHI 02] SHIM J.P., WARKENTIN M., COURTNEY J., POWER D., SHARDA R., CARLSSON C., "Past, present, and future of decision support technology", *Decision Support Systems*, vol. 33, no. 2, pp. 111–126, 2002.

[SIM 77] SIMON H., *The New Science of Management Decision*, Prentice-Hall, Englewood-Cliffs, NJ, 1977.

[SMO 02] SMOLIAR S., SPRAGUE R., "Communication and understanding for decision support", *Proceedings of the International Conference IFIP TC8/WG8.3*, Cork, Ireland, pp. 107–119, 2002.

[SOU 96] SOUBIE J.L., *Coopération et Systèmes à base de connaissances*, Accreditation to Supervise Research, University Paul Sabatier, Toulouse, November 1996.

[SOU 98] SOUBIE J.L., "Modelling in cooperative knowledge based systems", *Proceedings of the International Conference (COOP'98)*, INRIA, Cannes, France, pp. 45–48, May 1998.

[SOU 05] SOUBIE J.L., ZARATÉ P., "Use of cooperative systems for distributed decision making", *Group Decision and Negotiation Journal*, vol. 14, no. 2, pp. 147–158, 2005.

[SPE 90] SPERBER D., WILSON D., *La Pertinence*, Odile Jacob, Paris, 1990.

[SPR 82] SPRAGUE R., CARLSON E., *Building Effective Decision Support Systems*, Prentice-Hall, Englewood Cliffs, NJ, 1982.

[STA 00] STAL-LE-CARDINAL J., Etude de dysfonctionnement des processus de décision, application au choix d'acteur, Doctoral Thesis, Ecole Centrale Paris, 2000.

[TÉT 02] TÉTARD F., Managers, fragmentation of working time, and information systems, Doctoral Thesis, Abo Akademi University, Turku, Finland, 2002.

[TEU 01] TEULIER-BOURGINE R., ZARATÉ P., "Vers une problématique de l'aide à la décision utilisant les connaissances", *Actes de la Conférence en Ingénierie des Connaissances (IC'01)*, Grenoble, France, pp. 147–166, 2001.

[THO 01] THOMASSEN M., LORENZEN M., "The dynamic costs of coordination and specialization: production activities and learning processes in the Danish construction and furniture industries", *DRUID Nelson and Winter Conference*, Aalborg, Denmark, 12–15 June 2001.

[TSO 08] TSOUKIAS A., "From decision theory to decision aiding methodology", *European Journal of Operational Research*, vol. 187, pp. 138–161, 2008.

[WIN 94] WINNER M., RAY K., *Collaboration Handbook: Creating, Sustaining and Enjoying the Journey*, AMHERST H. (ed.), Wilder Foundation, St Paul, MN, 1994.

[ZAC 90] ZACHARY W.W., ROBERSTON S.P., "Introduction", in ZACHARY W.W., ROBERSTON S.P., BLACK J.B. (eds), *Cognition, Computing and Cooperation*, Ablex Publishing Corporation, Norwood, 1990.

[ZAR 91a] ZARATÉ P., Conception et Mise en œuvre de Systèmes Interactifs d'Aide à la Décision: Application à l'élaboration des plannings de repos du personnel navigant, Doctoral Thesis, University of Paris Dauphine, France, 1991.

[ZAR 91b] ZARATÉ P., "The process of designing a DSS: a case study in planning management", *European Journal of Operational Research*, vol. 55, pp. 394–402, 1991.

[ZAR 02] ZARATÉ P., "Collective decision making: which supports for which situations?" *Proceedings of the International Conference IFIP TC8/WG8.3*, 4–7 July, Cork, Ireland, pp. 96–106, 2002.

[ZAR 04] ZARATÉ P., SOUBIE J.L., An overview of supports for collective decision making", *Journal of Decision Systems*, vol. 13, no. 2, pp. 211–221, 2004.

[ZAR 05a] ZARATÉ P., MUNOZ M., SOUBIE J.L., HOUÉ R., "Knowledge management systems: a process oriented view", *Cybernetics and Systems Analysis*, vol. 41, no. 2, pp. 274–277, March 2005.

[ZAR 05b] ZARATÉ P., SOUBIE J.L., BUI T., "Experiment of a group multi-criteria decision support system for distributed decision making processes", *Proceedings of the International Conference HICSS38*, Hawaii, 3–6 January 2005.

List of websites

– Arc92 (2004): http://www.kindlingapp.com

– BrainReactions (2005): http://www.brainreactions.net

– BrightIdea (1999) http://www.brightidea.com/

– Campfire (1999): http://campfirenow.com

– CentralDesktop (2005): http://www.centraldesktop.com/

– CoVision (1985): http://www.webcouncil.com/wcapps

– Dialogr (2007): http://www.dialogr.com

– ExpertChoice (1983): http://www.expertchoice.com/

– Facilitate (1992): http://www.facilitate.com/company

– Groupsystems (1986): http://www.groupsystems.com/solutions

– Grouputer (1995): http://www.grouputer.com/

– Ideascale (2003): http://ideascale.com/

– Jamespot (2005): http://www.jamespot.pro/

– MeetingWorks (1994): http://www.meetingworks.com/html/meetingworks_tools.html

Index

A, B

application controller, 48, 49
Artificial Intelligence (AI), 23, 73, 75, 80
BrainReactions, 59, 87
brainstorming, 50, 84, 88
Brightidea, 59, 84

C

Campfire, 86
CentralDesktop, 59, 87
ChauffeurSort, 56
cognitive overflow syndrome, 7
collaborative decision, 13, 14, 29, 31-38, 51, 81, 84-86
collaborative engineering, 55
communication manager, 48, 49
complementary cooperation, 27, 28, 29, 75
Computer Supported Collaborative Work (CSCW), 31, 50, 57

CooP, 15, 16, 18, 50
cooperation management module, 47, 91
Cooperative Decision Support System (CDSS), 66
Cooperative design approach, 56
Cooperative DSS, 49, 92
Cooperative multi-agent system, 62
Cooperative system, 57
CrowBar, 56

D

Data Base Management System, 67
DataBase Management System (DBMS), 41
data warehouse, 42, 43
dataweb, 43
Decision Support System (DSS), 39, 49, 50
Decision Time Line (DTL), 2, 3
decisional information system, 42